GOD'S ABRAHAMIC COVENANTS WITH ISRAEL AND THE CHURCH

BIBLICAL ROAD MAP OF RECONCILIATION

Restoring the Altars, Foundations, and Pillars on
The Mountains of Israel

TOM HESS

GOD'S ABRAHAMIC COVENANTS WITH ISRAEL AND THE CHURCH
—BIBLICAL ROAD MAP OF RECONCILIATION
Restoring the Altars, Foundations and Pillars on The
Mountains of Israel

ISBN: 965-7193-13-3

Published by
Progressive Vision Publishing
P.O. Box 31393
Jerusalem 91313
Israel

This book has been written, typeset, and printed in Israel in agreement with Isaiah 2:3:

"The law will go forth out of Zion, and the word of the LORD from Jerusalem."

Unless otherwise noted, Scripture quotations in this book are taken from the Holy Bible, NEW INTERNATIONAL VERSION. Copyright © 1973, 1978, 1984 by International Bible Society. Used by permission of International Bible Society.

All bracketed notes inside biblical quotes are the author's comments.

ENDORSEMENTS

God bless you, Tom Hess, for this inspired and inspiring book! God bless you for being faithful to the Word of God and to the true calling and destiny of the House of Israel. May your book find its way into many Jewish, Christian and Muslim hearts, and may it move us all a little closer to the era of peace for which we yearn and pray.

> Moshe Aumann, citizen of Jerusalem, Israel
> Minister (Ret.), Ministry of Foreign Affairs of Israel
> Editor of *"Christians & Israel"* Quarterly
> Author of *Conflict and Connection: The Jewish-Christian-Israel Triangle* (2003)

My friend, Tom Hess, ardent Christian activist, has for fifteen years been leading representatives of some two-hundred nations in a round-the-clock prayer vigil on the Mount of Olives in Jerusalem for reconciliation between Jews, Christians and Muslims. His new book, *God's Abrahamic Covenant with Israel,* is a passionate affirmation of his faith in biblical prophecies of the restoration of Israel in its ancient land.

> Rabbi Joshua O. Haberman
> Rabbi Emeritus, Washington Hebrew Congregation
> Former President, Rabbinical Council, Washington D.C.
> Citizen of Jerusalem, Israel, and Washington, D.C.

The world leaders are in confusion and make erroneous decisions for Israel because they do not understand the covenants that God has made with Abraham. No matter how many "peace treaties" Israel signs there will be no peace for Israel if it does not take into consideration the truths of this book which are based on the Old Testament, which is God's Covenant with Israel. This book needs to be in the hands of every world leader and politician who "messes" with Israel. The media needs to understand these eternal covenant promises also.

If they read this book, they might not be so negatively opinionated against Israel. Give this book to your politicians. Buy it by the dozen and put them in the hands of those who try to make decisions concerning Israel. If you do this the blood of the Israelis will not be on your hands.

Gwen R. Shaw
Founder and President of End-Time Handmaidens, U.S.A.

God's Abrahamic Covenants with Israel and The Church is an excellent book that gives prophetic clarity from the Word of God on how God's covenants with the land of Israel and the Jewish people through Abraham, Isaac, and Jacob/Israel are for today, time-space history, and forever. This book also shows how the Arabs can be greatly blessed if they recognize God's covenants with Israel through Abraham and are willing to enter into the fullness of God's blessing by embracing God's will. If you want to understand the political situation in Israel from God's perspective through His word and have understanding of how to pray and work for peace in Israel and the Middle East, this book is a must for you.

Mike Bickle
International House of Prayer for All Nations
Kansas City, Missouri, U.S.A.

From a heart of love for Israel comes another masterpiece, a book that captures the gravity of the contracts the God of the Bible made with the people of Israel. This book will be the key to anyone understanding the unique nature of the relationship between God, the people and the land of the Bible. Enjoy a journey through the heart of God that leads even to the solution for the present day Middle East crisis.

Dr. Myles Munroe
Nassau, Bahamas

In his desire to be a bridge-builder between Jewish people and Christians, Tom Hess' latest book offers a biblical perspective to the "Road Map" for Middle East peace. Identifying four significant altars of covenant between God and the people of Israel—Shechem, Hebron, Beth El and Jerusalem—Tom expressed belief is that the enemies of Israel, i.e., Islam, seek to uproot God's covenant people from the very sites where God made covenant with them. Each biblical altar site is a foundation and pillar of the house of Israel and are presently under Islamic rule and proposed to be the foundations of an Islamic Palestinian State. According to Tom these locations are the greatest centers of conflict in Judea and Samaria, Israel today: Nablus (Shechem), Ramallah (Beth El), Kiryat Arba (Hebron), and Mt. Moriah (Jerusalem).

Jane Hansen
President/CEO
Aglow International

John 8:32 tells us that we shall know the truth and the truth shall set us free. The truth about God as a God of Covenants has recently been circulating in the body of Messiah. However, such a detailed exposition on the topic is made available to us thanks to someone who truly has devoted himself wholly to the idea of revealing the God of Israel.

As a gentile believer, I wish to personally thank Tom Hess for this excellent work, for you make me see my Master, my Lord and my God as a faithful, reliable, covenant-keeping God.

May this work bring understanding for all the peoples of our world in the way they view Israel and the Arabs amidst the chaos of today's reality in the Middle East.

Thank you brother Tom!

Sunday Adelaja
Senior Pastor of the Embassy of the Blessed Kingdom of
God for all Nations
Kiev, Ukraine

Once again Tom Hess has packed a book from cover to cover with information, illustrations and insights that unlock a unique understanding of God's way of shalom for His people. Packed with biblical references, *God's Abrahamic Covenant with Israel and The Church* reveals the true and only biblical peace plan, not only for Israel and the Middle East, but ultimately the whole world.

Dr. Dick Eastman
International President
Every Home for Christ

I am captivated by the insights God continues to give Tom Hess about God's covenants with Israel. Tom is being greatly used of God in awakening the world to the place God has for Israel in our day, and of how Isaac's sons and Ishmael's sons can only be brought together through the Messiah, descendant of Isaac and Jacob. Tom hits at the core of the problem by showing that the chief trouble spots in the Middle East today are the very places where Abraham, then later Isaac and Jacob, built altars to God and where

God renewed His covenant to them and their descendants, both literally and spiritually. This understanding is significant.

Don Finto
Author of *Your People Shall be My People*
USA

God's Abrahamic Covenants with Israel and The Church is a scriptural expose emphasizing the covenantal faithfulness of The God of Israel who has given His promise. As you read this book you will realize that God's Word will come to pass and, in spite of any opposition, God's Road Map for Israel and the Middle East will come to pass.

James (Jim) W. Goll
Author of *The Lost Art of Intercession* and *Exodus Cry*
USA

Tom Hess presents here a biblical Roadmap, built on the comprehensive testimony of the Word of God, which stands over every human or political Roadmap of our day. It looks like a dream and it *is* a dream, but it is the very dream of God Himself, for whom nothing is impossible. This book will be a stumbling block for many. Without humbling ourselves and taking every thought captive to the obedience of Christ, we will fail to embrace its message. It's not about Israelis and Arabs, the USA, the UN or the EU. The question is: Do we accept that the God of Israel is God? Let us pray that this message will reach out even to people behind closed doors who carry responsibilities in this current Roadmap process.

Geri Keller
Switzerland

Tom Hess writes with much insight and experience. As one who knows Israel and who has lived there many years he clearly explains the situation. Without a biblical-historical perspective on Israel the world is tempted to accept what looks to be the quickest and easiest solution to the problem in the Middle East. Tom Hess shows us how shallow and dangerous the secular solutions are and how vital it is to understand the biblical covenants and their validity today. He also points to a solution that is not biased, but includes both Arabs and Jews. The book has a wealth of information and scripture references valuable for anyone who wants to dig deeper in this very important subject.

Ulf Ekman
Word of Life Church and Ministries
Uppsala-Jerusalem

GOD'S ABRAHAMIC COVENANTS WITH ISRAEL AND THE CHURCH

BIBLICAL ROAD MAP OF RECONCILIATION

Restoring the Altars, Foundations, and Pillars on
The Mountains of Israel

DEDICATION

It has been an honour and joy to write *God's Abrahamic Covenants with Israel and The Church* by the revelation and inspiration of the Covenant God of Israel, THE ONE TRUE GOD. I wholeheartedly dedicate *God's Abrahamic Covenants with Israel and The Church* to the Covenant God of Israel, who keeps his covenants and shows mercy to all who walk before him with all their heart and to the chosen people of Israel hoping that they will fully believe in and trust in and love their awesome God who is their only hope.

Hear, O Israel: The LORD our God, the LORD is one. Love the LORD your God with all your heart and with all your soul and with all your strength (Deuteronomy 6:4, 5).

I also want to dedicate it to two specific communities: first to Jews who have sacrificed the comforts of the USA and other nations, Tel Aviv and other places in Israel to stand with the God of Israel and His Abrahamic covenants with the land in the places of the altars, foundations and pillars in the heartland of Israel:

Families like my friends Yossi Kapach, a former mayor whose son was killed in 1987 by Muslim terrorists at their home in BETH EL, but continues to faithfully stand; Rabbi Benny Elon, the Minister of Tourism, Chaim Silberstein, and others who are standing with God's Abrahamic covenants in Beth El, where God promised the whole land to Abraham and Jacob, where Jacob's ladder was the gateway to heaven, and where Jacob's name was changed to Israel forever;

Pinchas Fuchs who left the comforts of the USA and suffers from stress and nervousness, but continues to stand in SHECHEM and ELON MOREH, where the land was first promised to Abraham, after seeing four close friends murdered by terrorists; Menachem and Tova Gilboa, who were almost killed by terrorists and at another

xi

time had their hotel bombed in ARIEL, who have a deep faith in and love for the God of Israel, His covenants and land, and still continue to stand;

David Rubin, the Mayor of SHILO, who emigrated from the USA and who barely escaped death when he and his son were shot and were miraculously delivered and healed by the covenant keeping God of Israel;

Continuing to stand with the covenants of Israel are all the children and grandchildren who returned to Kefar Etzion in the hills of Hebron after all the fathers were martyred there in 1948 while helping to liberate Jerusalem and who continue to stand for the covenants of Israel;

Gary Cooperberg and his family, who made *Aliyah* from the USA and who now lives in KIRYAT ARBA/HEBRON where terrorists have killed dozens of his friends there. He is also, at his own expense, encouraging American Jews to make *Aliyah* to Kiryat Arba and Hebron; and

Mayor Ron Nachman of ARIEL, who has a prayer-room in his office for Christians, has been attacked by both Jews and Muslims; Dr. Newman (the best doctor I have ever had), my hygienist, and Rabbi Riskin from EPHRATA; and my friend Mayor Benny Kashriel of MA'ALE ADUMIM who wants to rebuild the Good Samaritan Inn, from the time and story of Jesus, as a sign of brotherhood between Jews and Christians.

All these heroes of faith in the Covenant God of Israel are holding up the pillars of the House of Israel and defending the Abrahamic Covenants in the places where they were made.

All these heroes of faith in the Covenant God of Israel are defending the Abrahamic Covenants in the places where they were made and are standing for the foundations and holding up the pillars of the House of Israel.

Most nations and Muslims mock and ridicule them, including many Israelis and Christians. Even some of the more recent governments of Israel have abandoned them. They continue to faithfully stand for and defend the Abrahamic covenants in the places where they were made by standing for the foundations and pillars of the House of Israel. There are a few bad extremists among them as with most movements, but most are faithful to the Covenants of Abraham. We honor them for their faithfulness and courage as present day Joshuas and Calebs.

Hearing that Jesus had silenced the Sadducees, the Pharisees got together. One of them, an expert in the law, tested him with this question: "Teacher, which is the Greatest Commandment in the law?"

Jesus replied: " 'Love the Lord your God with all your heart and with all your soul and with all your mind.' This is the first and greatest commandment. And the second is like it: 'Love your neighbor as yourself.' All the Law and the prophets hang on these two commandments" (Matthew 22:34-40).

Secondly, this book is dedicated and written in honor of all the Arabs who, against all odds by sheer faith, are standing for the God of Israel and His Abrahamic Covenants. They are being changed by Jesus to love the God of Israel and their neighbors as themselves in the natural and spiritual as they are also natural sons of Abraham. I thank the God of Israel for the Arabs who God has saved throughout the Arab world and in Israel and now reject all forms of replacement theology that tries to replace Israel with the Church and stand for the Abrahamic Covenants along with the Jews:

Afeef, an Arab Moabite from JORDAN, who says like Ruth, "May your people be my people, your God, my God. Where you lie, I will lie." He is teaching against replacement theology to the Arabs and was rejected by some of his friends for his stance;

Yoseph from IRAQ who continues to firmly stand with the Abrahamic covenants and has been sending missiles of love to the Jews in Israel for the last twelve years counteracting the missiles of the now fallen regime of Sadam Hussein;

George who was born in Jerusalem, now living in Amman, JORDAN, who led a time of affirming the covenant of Isaiah 19: 23-25 with Benjamin, a Jewish leader in Jerusalem, just before *Yom Kippur* 1994. A few hours after affirming the covenant, an earthquake occurred centered in Amman, Jordan, and Jerusalem, Israel. This was a sign of answered prayers and a first fruit of God's of Isaiah 19:23-25;

Bassam from JERUSALEM, whose house was stolen by Muslims, who is standing for the reconciliation and salvation of the Jews and Arabs in Jerusalem through the God of Israel, His covenant for Jerusalem, and for the other covenant cities of the Abrahamic covenant;

Shadi from TAYIBE, a village next to Beth El, who courageously stands for Israel, the places of covenants, and reconciliation for all;

Arabs like Emil from EGYPT and Mokhtar from TUNISIA who faithfully stand with the Abrahamic covenants against all odds. These men are present day heroes like those of old: Naaman of Syria, Ruth of Jordan, the Good Samaritan in Israel, and Sadat of Egypt, who are preparing the way for the highway from Egypt to Israel and Assyria (Isaiah 19:23-25; Psalm 87) and Messiah's coming.

To see real peace/*shalom*/*salaam*, Bible-believing Jews and Christians (including Arab-Christians) must realize that neither one of our communities have all the truth alone. We need to embrace one another and our God-given covenant as natural and spiritual sons of Abraham.

May the covenant-keeping God of Israel raise up millions of Jews and Arabs to stand with the Abrahamic Covenants so that His peace will come in the natural and spiritual to all the natural and spiritual children of Abraham.

Tom Hess
Jerusalem & Caesarea, Israel
January 2004

Contents

PART I:
The Abrahamic Covenants

PART II:
Restoring the Four Covenantal Altars
The Foundations and Pillars of the House of Israel

PART III:
The Abrahamic Covenant with Believing Israel
and Believing Gentiles

PART IV:
The Covenants and the Land

PART V:
Towards Peace

APPENDIX
Watchmen's Materials

The Abrahamic Covenants

Chapter 1

God's Abrahamic Covenants with Israel Forever

Biblical Highway (Road Map)

This book, God's Abrahamic Covenants with Israel and The Church—Biblical Road Map of Reconciliation, is written to both the Jewish and Christian communities as was my first book, *Let My People Go!*, as a type of dialogue between Jews and Christians. The purpose of this book is to encourage the people of Israel, the Jewish people, to believe and trust in their God, the covenant God of Israel and His covenants with Abraham, and for Arab-Christians and Christians worldwide to do the same. As the children of Abraham by faith, together we all need to look to Abraham our father (Isaiah 51).

God's covenants with Abraham came before the law was given to Moses on Sinai, showing God deeded and covenanted the Land of Israel to the Jewish people by Jacob's name being changed to Israel. Its timing also shows that the Abrahamic Covenant continues through the time of the law, still continues today, and will continue FOREVER. Not only Jews, but also all believers in the God of Israel, including Arabs, can become partakers in the Abrahamic Covenants by faith in the God of Israel. In the New (Testament) Covenant, Galatians 3:29 says all true Christians are children of Abraham by faith! While this does not give all Christians worldwide the right to be citizens of Israel, it does graft them into the olive tree as wild olive branches joining the natural branches as part of the commonwealth of Israel spiritually.

1

The Mosaic Covenant (Exodus 20:1-17) and the New Covenant (Jeremiah 31:30-34) in no way replace God's covenants with Abraham that are promised FOREVER. Christians must also remember that Jesus, their king, is from the lineage of David the Jewish King of Israel and of Father Abraham. We must stand together and honor our biblical roots in the Abrahamic covenant. This book is about faith in the God of Israel and His Abrahamic covenants in the Bible, not about politics.

If you watch the world media about Israel and the Arab Middle East, it is easy to be greatly confused. Reading *God's Abrahamic Covenants with Israel and The Church—Biblical Road Map of Reconciliation* will give clarification to Jerusalem, Israel, and the Middle East from God's perspective. It will help you see events through His eyes related to the eternal covenants with Israel and the heartland of Israel today—biblically called Judea and Samaria. On the mountains of Israel in Beth El, Israel was born when Jacob's name was changed to Israel. There, God promised the heartland of Israel, Judea and Samaria and all the Land of Israel to the Jewish people FOREVER as an EVERLASTING COVENANT-POSSESSION.

> **The LORD said to Abram after Lot had parted from him, "Lift up your eyes from where you are and look north and south, east and west. All the land that you see I will give you and your offspring FOREVER. I will make your offspring like the dust of the earth, so that if anyone could count the dust, then your offspring could be counted. Go, walk through the length and breadth of the land, for I am giving it to you" (Genesis 13: 14-17, Emphasis added).**

From where God showed this to Abraham in Beth El, on a clear day one can see to Mount Hermon, to the Mediterranean Sea, to

Jordan, and to the hills of Hebron. In Beth El, God promised the land to Abraham. Beth El is the center of the heart of what is now being proposed for an Islamic Palestinian State by the nations of the world. You can see Mount Hermon, Shechem, Jerusalem, and to Hebron—all the places of covenant and covenant altars.

God says:

> I will establish my covenant as an **EVERLASTING COVENANT** between me and you and your descendants after you for the generations to come, to be your God and the God of your descendants after you. The whole land of Canaan, where you are now an alien, I will give you as an **EVERLASTING POSSESSION** to you and your descendants after you; and I will be their God (**Genesis 17:7, 8, Emphasis added**).

> Then God said to Abraham, "Your wife Sarah will bear you a son, and you will call him Isaac. I will establish my covenant with him as an **EVERLASTING COVENANT** for his descendants after him. And as for Ishmael, I have heard you: I will surely bless him; I will make him fruitful and will greatly increase his numbers. He will be the father of twelve rulers, and I will make him into a great nation" (**Genesis 17:19, 20, Emphasis added**).

> Remember your servants Abraham, Isaac, and Israel, to whom you swore by your own self: I will make your descendants as numerous as the stars in the sky and I will give your descendants all this land I promised them, and it will be their inheritance **FOREVER** (**Exodus 32:13, Emphasis added**).

3

He remembers his COVENANT FOREVER, the word he commanded, for a thousand generations, the covenant he made with Abraham, the oath he swore with Isaac. He confirmed it to Jacob as a decree, to Israel as an EVERLASTING COVENANT: "To you I will give the land of Canaan as the portion you will inherit" (I Chronicles 16: 15-18, Emphasis added)).

For to us a child is born, to us a son is given, and the government will be on his shoulders. And he will be called Wonderful Counselor, Mighty God, Everlasting Father, Prince of Peace. Of the increase of his government and peace there will be no end. He will reign on David's throne and over his kingdom, establishing and upholding it with justice and righteousness from that time on and FOREVER. The zeal of the LORD Almighty will accomplish this (Isaiah 9:6, 7, Emphasis added)).

Then the man brought me to the gate facing east, and I saw the glory of the God of Israel coming from the east. His voice was like the roar of rushing waters, and the land was radiant with his glory. The vision I saw was like the vision I had seen when he came to destroy the city and like the vision I had seen by the Kebar River, and I fell face down. The glory of the LORD entered the temple through the gate facing east. Then the Spirit lifted me up and brought me into the inner court and the glory of the LORD filled the temple.

While the man was standing beside me, I heard someone speaking to me from inside the temple. He said: "Son of Man, this [land] is the

4

place of my throne and the place for the soles of my feet [on the Temple Mount]. This is where I will live among the Israelites FOREVER (Ezekiel 43:1-7, Emphasis added).

Understanding God's covenants with Abraham and Israel in Genesis 15 on Mount Hermon and the four altars that Abraham built in Shechem, Hebron, Beth El, and Jerusalem and understanding God's purpose of restoration in these last days will give perspective and keys to help clarify events in our days and to unlock the foundations and pillars of God's peace plan in Messiah. God wants to establish His peace plan in Israel and the Arab Middle East.

God is a covenant-keeping God both for Israel and the Church. If God did not keep his covenants with Israel there would be no reason for Him to keep them with the Church. The God of Israel made covenants with Abraham, Jacob (whose name was changed to Israel), and David, King of Israel, at the places where the four altars of covenant were built.

God is a covenant-keeping God both for Israel and the Church. If God did not keep his covenants with Israel there would be no reason for Him to keep them with the Church.

Abraham, Jacob, and David made covenants with the God of Israel by building altars and purchasing land in these places over three thousand years ago, which is more than two thousand years before Islam shows up in history. This clearly shows that the land was covenanted to them by God and that he has ordained the Jewish people to be stewards over Judea and Samaria, the heartland of Israel, including the altars, foundations, and pillars established in Shechem, Hebron, Beth El, and Jerusalem.

Heathen nations and some Muslims call Judea and Samaria, the heartland of Israel, "Occupied Territories" and the "West Bank." This very heartland is where some Muslims and many other nations want to establish an Islamic Palestinian State. All Jews and Bible-believing Christians need to reject the lies of the nations and embrace the God of Israel and His covenants. Unless God intervenes due to the prayers, fasting and warning of the people, the USA and other nations will be judged for dividing up the land of Israel (Joel 3:2).

Each Passover for ten years, we have built altars in Shechem, Beth El, Hebron, and Jerusalem. Since Passover 2002,

The enemies of Israel trying to destroy the foundations and knock downthe pillars of the house of Israel and cause the Jewish people to break covenants with their God.

when I visited Beth El and realized Arafat is one kilometer away, my eyes were opened wider. I began to see the fuller significance of the four places where Abraham, Isaac and Jacob (whose name was changed to Israel) built altars. I began to realize what the enemies of Israel are trying to do: They are trying to destroy the foundations and knock down the pillars of the house of Israel and cause the Jewish people to break covenants with their God in the very places where God made covenants with them.

All replacement theologies and ideologies are born out of rebellion against the Covenant God of Israel and the Abrahamic covenants. Those who deny God's just choice of Isaac and Jacob (whose name was changed to Israel) and say that God chose Ishmael or other replacements instead of Isaac, are enemies of peace. This is because they worship another god, a moon god, not the One True Covenant God of Israel. Islam teaches that the whole world, especially the heartland of Israel, should submit to Allah and Islamic rule. It is not a matter of giving the Palestinian people land to live on. It is not as in South Africa where the human rights issue of land for people to live on is the problem. No! In Israel, we are dealing with something that has to do with the kingdoms of darkness against the kingdom of our Lord and His Messiah. We are dealing with covenants. Those in the nations need to understand that we are dealing with the covenants of the God of Israel and His land and His people.

6

Terrorists and all people that do not understand God's covenants are trying to drive the Jewish people out of this land (what they call settlements) promised to them by God. That is what terrorism in Israel is all about, trying to uproot God's covenant people and lay the foundations of Islam in the places where God made covenants with His people. It is no accident that Arafat has for years lived in Ramallah, one kilometer from Beth El where Jacob's name was changed to Israel. Islam and Arafat have been demanding that Beth El, Shilo, and all the places of God's covenants be evacuated so that the foundations of Israel are destroyed and another foundation can replace God's covenants and the Jewish communities of Beth El and Shilo. The same is true in Shechem, Hebron, and Jerusalem.

It is time for the Jewish nation of Israel to turn back to the God of Israel and believe the Bible, trust in Him, and believe in His covenants. It is time for all Bible-believing Arab-Christians and Bible-believing Christians worldwide to stand in solidarity with God's covenants made with the people and the land of Israel, which are also our covenants as the children of Abraham by faith. God's covenants with Abraham belong not only to all Jews, but also to Christians worldwide, as they were made both naturally and spiritually in these places, as we are all called to be children of Abraham by faith. A house united will stand; a house divided will fall.

That is what terrorism in Israel is all about, trying to uproot God's covenant people and lay the foundations of Islam in the places where God made covenants with His people.

We believe that it is God's will and desire that Jews and Arabs will cooperate with Him not to build fences to be divided, but to be reconciled to the God of Israel and each other, through the Prince of Peace (Isaiah 9:6). God's purpose is that Jew and Arab—Egypt, Israel, and Assyria—will worship Him together as a blessing in the midst of the earth (Isaiah 19:19-25) in the center of the Middle East (Israel is the center and place of the five altars built by Abraham). It took a lot of humility for Naaman, the Syrian

7

Chief of Staff, to kneel before a Jewish prophet, but when he did, war ceased and peace came (see II Kings 5:6). Until the Arabs reject lies and support God's covenants with the land and Jewish people, real peace will not come. If God's peace plan is not established in these areas there will not be real peace. If salvation and reconciliation is established in Mount Hermon, Shechem, Beth El, Hebron, and Jerusalem, then shalom/salaam will not only come to Jerusalem, but also to Mount Hermon, Judea and Samaria and all nations. All nations could enter into God's Abrahamic covenants through the Prince of Peace, King of Israel, and stream into Zion.

It is time for Jewish people, Bible-believing Arab-Christians and Bible believing Christian worldwide to renew the covenant with God and the land as Joshua did.

Now it is imperative that all Jews and Bible-believing Arab-Christians stand together with God's Abrahamic covenants with the Jewish communities in Judea and Samaria. Without these Abrahamic Covenants the foundations of the Jews and Israel would not exist, but also the Abrahamic foundations of the Christian Church worldwide. The New (Testament) Covenant says all Christians are also children of Abraham by faith and heirs spiritually according to the covenantal promise to Abraham.

It is true that injustices have been done by Jews towards Arabs that need to be rectified. However, we must stand and not allow a hijacking of God's covenantal land, purposes, and people. We must embrace our destiny with the God of Israel and His covenants with the land of Israel. I say as Joshua did, "As for me and my household we will serve the Lord, the God of Israel." It is time for Jewish people, Bible-believing Arab-Christians and Bible-believing Christians worldwide to renew the covenant with God and the land as Joshua did. The Jews, Arab-Christians, and Christians worldwide together need to do justice, love mercy and walk humbly before God (Micah 6:8). Justice is honoring God's word and Him as a just God. It is just that God chose to covenant the Land of Israel to the Jewish people FOREVER. It is also very important that the

Jewish people treat Arabs with justice as the Bible says, "Justice and righteousness are the foundations of God's throne." May justice roll on like a river and righteousness like a never-ending stream (Amos 5:24) in the places where God made covenants with Abraham: in Egypt, Israel, Assyria, and worldwide. For the fruit of justice will be peace and the effect of righteousness, security and trust (Isaiah 32: 17) preparing the way for Messiah.

We need to pray that the veil over the eyes of many Jews and Christians in regard to the Abrahamic Covenants will be removed. Jews must reject the lies that the God of Israel does not exist and that the USA and their multi-billion dollar loans are more important than the Covenant God of Israel and His promises. In Exodus 20: 3 God says, "You shall have no other gods before me." Christians must reject the lie of replacement theology that says the New (Testament) Covenant and the Church completely replaced all the Old (Testament) Abrahamic Covenants and Israel. Christians must understand Romans 11:28, 29. God says as far as election (the Jewish people) they are loved because of the fathers (patriarchs) and that God's gifts and callings are irrevocable. Together as the natural and spiritual children of Abraham, we pray that we will honor and stand with the Abrahamic Covenants to see the fullness of the natural and spiritual restoration of Israel, Egypt, Assyria, and the Church worldwide.

Together as the natural and spiritual children of Abraham, we pray that we will honor and stand with the Abrahamic Covenants to see the fullness of the natural and spiritual restoration of Israel, Egypt, Assyria, and the Church worldwide.

My prayer is that this book will help kindle a fire among Jews, Arab-Christians and Christians worldwide; a fire to repent and together renew the Abrahamic covenants with the Covenant God of Israel preparing to see Ezekiel 36 restored in the natural, and Ezekiel 37 in the spiritual, to see the way prepared for the coming of the Jewish Messiah, the Messiah of all the earth.

Maybe the Jews should again give some money for the land as Jacob, David and Abraham did, even though the land is biblically,

9

covenantally and inherently Israel's. This is not like the land of Native Americans in the USA or like the South African problem, because God had no biblical and everlasting covenants with the Europeans who claimed the lands and settled them. God wants the Jews to stand on the covenants He made with them through Father Abraham, Isaac and Jacob-Israel. Only by this, along with the Arabs honoring the covenants God made with the Jews through Abraham, will the Arabs receive the full blessing that is their redemptive purpose and destiny. Jews and Arabs will both be blessed and a blessing in the midst of the earth.

This book is mostly the word of the God of the Bible. Within this book are seventy scriptures about the God of Israel in chapter two. In chapter ten, six hundred scripture verses are included about God's covenants with the land of Israel reinforcing the ones He made with Abraham, Jacob-Israel, and their descendants forever. The covenants God made with Abraham, Isaac, and Jacob-Israel were in and for THE WHOLE LAND OF ISRAEL, but specifically made in the heartland of Israel, the Mountains of Israel, the West Bank of the Jordan River, biblical Judea and Samaria—Mount Hermon, Shechem, Beth El, Hebron, and Jerusalem. These covenants are FOREVER.

> O LORD God of Israel, there is no God like thee in heaven, nor in the earth, which keepest covenant [forever], and shows mercy unto thy servants, that walk before thee with all their hearts (II Chronicles 6:14 KJV, Emphasis added).

Chapter 2

Seventy Scriptures About The Covenant God of Israel

The following scriptures are for all of God's people, both Jews and Christians, to read and meditate on to grow in faith in the Covenant God of Israel and His covenants. Reading this second chapter of scriptures is very important to more fully understand this book.

Exodus 5:1
Afterwards Moses and Aaron went to Pharaoh and said, "This is what the LORD, the God of Israel, says: 'Let my people go, so that they may hold a festival to me in the desert.' "

Exodus 34:23
Three times a year all your men are to appear before the Sovereign LORD, the God of Israel.

Joshua 8:30, 31
Then Joshua built on Mount Ebal an altar to the LORD, the God of Israel, as Moses the servant of the LORD had commanded the Israelites.

Joshua 14:13, 14
Then Joshua blessed Caleb son of Jephunneh and gave him Hebron as his inheritance. So Hebron has belonged to Caleb son of Jephunneh the Kenizzite ever since, because he followed the LORD, the God of Israel, wholeheartedly.

Joshua 24:2

Joshua said to all the people, "This is what the LORD, the God of Israel, says: 'Long ago your forefathers, including Terah the father of Abraham and Nahor, lived beyond the River and worshipped other gods.' "

Joshua 24:23-26

"Now then," said Joshua, "throw away the foreign gods that are among you and yield your hearts to the LORD, the God of Israel."

And the people said to Joshua, "We will serve the LORD our God and obey him."

On that day Joshua made a covenant for the people, and there at Shechem he drew up for them decrees and laws. And Joshua recorded these things in the Book of the Law of God. Then he took a large stone and set it up there under the oak near the holy place of the LORD.

Judges 5:5

The mountains quaked before the LORD, the One of Sinai, before the LORD, the God of Israel.

Ruth 2:12

Boaz replied, "May the LORD repay you [Ruth] for what you have done. May you be richly rewarded by the LORD, the God of Israel, under whose wings you have come to take refuge."

I Samuel 1:17

Eli answered, "Go in peace, and may the God of Israel grant you [Hannah] what you have asked of him."

I Samuel 2:30

Therefore the LORD, the God of Israel, declares: "I promised that your house and your father's house would minister before me forever." But now the LORD declares: "Far be it from me! Those who honour me I will honour, but those who despise me will be disdained."

I Samuel 20:12

Then Jonathan said to David: "By the LORD, the God of Israel, I will surely sound out my father by this time the day after tomorrow! If he is favorably disposed towards you, will I not send you word and let you know?"

I Samuel 25:32-34

David said to Abigail, "Praise be to the LORD, the God of Israel, who has sent you today to meet me. May you be blessed for your good judgment and for keeping me from bloodshed this day and from avenging myself with my own hands. Otherwise, as surely as the LORD, the God of Israel, lives, who has kept me from harming you, if you had not come quickly to meet me, not one male belonging to Nabal would have been left alive by daybreak."

II Samuel 12:7

Then Nathan said to David, "You are the man! This is what the LORD, the God of Israel, says: 'I anointed you king over Israel, and I delivered you from the hand of Saul.' "

II Samuel 23:3-5

The God of Israel spoke, the Rock of Israel said to me [David]: "When one rules over men in righteousness, when he rules in the fear of God, he is like the light of morning at sunrise on a cloudless morning, like the brightness after rain that brings the grass from the earth."

Is not my house right with God? Has he not made with me an everlasting covenant arranged and secured in every part? Will he not bring to fruition my salvation and grant me every desire?

I Kings 1:30, 48

King David took an oath: "I will surely carry out today what I swore to you by the LORD, the God of Israel: Solomon your son shall be king after me, and he will sit on my throne in my place." And the king bowed and worshiped on his bed and said, "Praise be to the LORD, the God of Israel, who has allowed my eyes to see a successor on my throne today."

I Kings 8:15-17, 20, 21

Then he [Solomon] said: "Praise be to the LORD, the God of Israel, who with his own hand has fulfilled what he promised with his own mouth to my father David. For he said, 'Since the day I brought my people Israel out of Egypt, I have not chosen a city in any tribe of Israel to have a temple built for my Name to be there, but I have chosen David to rule my people Israel.'

My father David had it in his heart to build a temple for the Name of the LORD, the God of Israel...I have built the temple for the Name of the LORD, the God of Israel. I have provided a place there for the ark, in which is the covenant of the LORD that he made with our fathers when he brought them out of Egypt."

I Kings 8:23

O LORD, God of Israel, there is no God like you in heaven above or on earth below—you who keep your covenant of love with your servants who continue wholeheartedly in your way.

I Kings 8:25, 26

Now LORD, God of Israel, keep for your servant David my father the promises you made to him when you said, "You shall never fail to have a man to sit before me on the throne of Israel, if only your sons are careful in all they do to walk before me as you have done." And now, O God of Israel, let your word that you promised your servant David my father come true.

I Kings 17:1

Now Elijah the Tishbite, from Tishbe in Gilead, said to Ahab, "As the LORD, the God of Israel, lives, whom I serve, there will be neither dew nor rain in the next few years except at my word."

II Kings 14:25

He [Jerobam, son of Jehoash] was the one who restored the boundaries of Israel from Lebo Hamath to the sea of Arabah, in accordance with the word of the LORD, the God of Israel, spoken through his servant Jonah son of Amittai, the prophet from Gath Hepher.

II Kings 18:5

Hezekiah trusted in the LORD, the God of Israel. There was no-one like him among all the kings of Judah, either before him or after him. He held fast to the LORD and did not cease to follow him; he kept the commands the LORD had given Moses.

II Kings 19:15

And Hezekiah prayed to the LORD: "O LORD, God of Israel, enthroned between the cherubim, you alone are God over all the kingdoms of the earth. You have made heaven and earth."

II Kings 22:18, 19

Tell the king of Judah, who sent you to inquire of the LORD, "This is what the LORD, the God of Israel, says concerning the words you heard: 'Because your heart was responsive and you humbled yourself before the LORD when you heard what I have spoken against this place and its people, that they would become accursed and laid waste, and because you tore your robes and wept in my presence, I have heard you, declares the LORD.' "

I Chronicles 4:10

Jabez cried out to the God of Israel, "Oh, that you would bless me and enlarge my territory! Let your hand be with me, and keep me from harm so that I will be free from pain." And God granted his request.

I Chronicles 15:14

So the priests and Levites consecrated themselves in order to bring up the ark of the LORD, the God of Israel.

I Chronicles 16:4

He [David] appointed some of the Levites to minister before the ark of the LORD, to make petition, to give thanks, and to praise the LORD, the God of Israel.

I Chronicles 16:36

Praise be to the LORD, the God of Israel, from everlasting to everlasting. Then all the people said "Amen" and "Praise the LORD."

I Chronicles 17:23, 24

And now, LORD, let the promise you have made concerning your servant and his house be established forever. Do as you promised, so that it will be established and that your name will be great for ever. Then men will say, "The LORD Almighty, the God of Israel, is Israel's God!"

I Chronicles 22:6

Then he called for his son Solomon and charged him to build a house for the LORD, the God of Israel.

I Chronicles 23:25, 26

For David had said, "Since the LORD, the God of Israel, has granted rest to his people and has come to dwell in Jerusalem forever, the Levites no longer need to carry the tabernacle or any of the articles used in its service."

I Chronicles 24:19
This was their appointed order of ministering when they entered the temple of the LORD, according to the regulations prescribed for them by their forefather Aaron, as the LORD, the God of Israel, had commanded him.

I Chronicles 28:4
Yet the LORD, the God of Israel, chose me from my whole family to be king over Israel forever. He chose Judah as leader, and from the house of Judah he chose my family, and from my father's sons he was pleased to make me king over all Israel.

I Chronicles 29:10
David praised the LORD in the presence of the whole assembly, saying, "Praise be to you, O LORD, God of our father Israel, from everlasting to everlasting."

II Chronicles 2:12
And Hiram added: "Praise be to the LORD, God of Israel, who made heaven and earth! He has given King David a wise son, endowed with intelligence and discernment, who will build a temple for the LORD and a palace for himself."

II Chronicles 6:4
Then he [Solomon] said: "Praise be to the LORD, the God of Israel, who with his hands has fulfilled what he promised with his mouth to my father David."

II Chronicles 6:7, 10
My father David had it in his heart to build a temple for the Name of the LORD, the God of Israel. The LORD has kept the promise

he made. I have succeeded David my father and now I sit on the throne of Israel, just as the LORD promised, and I have built the temple for the Name of the LORD, the God of Israel.

II Chronicles 6:14-17

O LORD, God of Israel, there is no God like you in heaven or on earth—you who keep your covenant of love with your servants who continue wholeheartedly in your way. You have kept your promise to your servant David my father; with your mouth you have promised and with your hand you have fulfilled it—as it is today.

Now LORD, God of Israel, keep for your servant David my father the promises you made to him when you said, "You shall never fail to have a man to sit before me on the throne of Israel, if only your sons are careful in all they do to walk before me according to my law, as you have done." And now, O LORD, God of Israel, let your word that you have promised your servant David come true.

II Chronicles 11:16

Those from every tribe of Israel who set their hearts on seeking the LORD, the God of Israel, followed the Levites to Jerusalem to offer sacrifices to the LORD, the God of their fathers.

II Chronicles 13:5

Don't you know that the LORD, the God of Israel, has given the kingship of Israel to David and his descendants forever as a covenant of salt?

II Chronicles 15:4

But in their distress they turned to the LORD, the God of Israel, and sought him, and he was found by them.

II Chronicles 15:13-15

All who would not seek the LORD, the God of Israel, were to be put to death, whether small or great, man or woman. They took an oath to the LORD with loud acclamation, with shouting and with trumpets and horns. All Judah rejoiced about the oath because they had sworn it wholeheartedly. They sought God eagerly, and he was found by them. So the LORD gave them rest on every side.

II Chronicles 20:19
Then some Levites from the Kohathites and Korahites stood up and praised the LORD, the God of Israel, with a very loud voice.

II Chronicles 30:1, 5
Hezekiah sent word to all Israel and Judah and also wrote letters to Ephraim and Manasseh, inviting them to come to the temple of the LORD in Jerusalem and celebrate the Passover to the LORD, the God of Israel. They decided to send a proclamation throughout Israel, from Beersheba to Dan, calling the people to come to Jerusalem and celebrate the Passover to the LORD, the God of Israel.

II Chronicles 33:16
Then he [Manasseh] restored the altar of the LORD and sacrificed fellowship offerings and thank-offerings on it, and told Judah to serve the LORD, the God of Israel.

Ezra 7:6
This Ezra came up from Babylon. He was a teacher well versed in the Law of Moses, which the LORD, the God of Israel, had given.

Ezra 8:35
Then exiles who had returned from captivity sacrificed burnt offerings to the God of Israel.

Ezra 9:15
O LORD, God of Israel, you are righteous! We are left this day as a remnant. Here we are before you in our guilt, though because of it not one of us can stand in your presence.

Psalm 41:13

Praise be to the LORD, the God of Israel, from everlasting to everlasting. Amen and Amen.

Psalm 68:7-10

When you went out before your people, O God, when you marched through the wasteland, the earth shook, the heavens poured down rain, before God, the One of Sinai, before God, the God of Israel. You gave abundant showers, O God; you refreshed your weary inheritance. Your people settled in it, and from your bounty, O God, you provided for the poor.

Psalm 68:35

You are awesome, O God, in your sanctuary; the God of Israel gives power and strength to his people. Praise be to God!

Psalm 72:18, 19

Praise be to the LORD God, the God of Israel, who alone does marvelous deeds. Praise be to his glorious name for ever; may the whole earth be filled with his glory. Amen and Amen.

Psalm 106:48

Praise be to the LORD, the God of Israel, from everlasting to everlasting. Let all the people say, "Amen!" Praise the LORD.

Isaiah 24:14-16

They raise their voices, they shout for joy; from the west they acclaim the LORD's majesty. Therefore in the east give glory to the LORD; exalt the name of the LORD, the God of Israel, in the islands of the sea. From the ends of the earth we hear singing: "Glory to the Righteous One."

Isaiah 29:22-24

Therefore this is what the LORD, who redeemed Abraham, says

to the house of Jacob: "No longer will Jacob be ashamed; no longer will their faces grow pale. When they see among them their children, the work of my hands, they will keep my name holy; they will acknowledge the holiness of the Holy One of Jacob, and will stand in awe of the God of Israel.

Isaiah 37:15, 16
And Hezekiah prayed to the LORD: "O LORD Almighty, God of Israel, enthroned between the cherubim, you alone are God over all the kingdoms of the earth. You have made heaven and earth."

Isaiah 41:17-20
The poor and the needy search for water, but there is none; their tongues are parched with thirst. But I the LORD will answer them; I, the God of Israel, will not forsake them. I will make rivers flow on barren heights, and springs within the valleys. I will turn the desert into pools of water, and the parched ground into springs. I will put in the desert the cedar and the acacia, the myrtle and the olive. I will set pines in the wasteland, the fir and the cypress together, so that people may see and know, may consider and understand, that the hand of the LORD has done this, that the Holy One of Israel has created it.

Isaiah 45:15
Truly you are a God who hides himself, O God and Savior of Israel.

Isaiah 52:12
But you will not leave in haste or go in flight; for the LORD will go before you, the God of Israel will be your rear guard.

Jeremiah 7:3
This is what the LORD Almighty, the God of Israel, says: "Reform your ways and your actions, and I will let you live in this place."

Jeremiah 11:3

Tell them that this is what the LORD, the God of Israel, says: "Cursed is the man who does not obey the terms of this covenant—the terms I commanded your forefathers when I brought them out of Egypt, out of the iron-smelting furnace."

Jeremiah 23:2

Therefore this is what the LORD, the God of Israel, says to the shepherds who tend my people: "Because you have scattered my flock and driven them away and have not bestowed care on them, I will bestow punishment on you for the evil you have done," declares the LORD.

Jeremiah 31:23

This is what the LORD Almighty, the God of Israel, says: "When I bring them back from captivity, the people in the land of Judah and in its towns will once again use these words: 'The LORD bless you, O righteous dwelling, O sacred mountain.' "

Jeremiah 32:14, 15

This is what the LORD Almighty, the God of Israel, says: "Take these documents, both the sealed and unsealed copies of the deed of purchase, and put them in a clay jar so that they will last a long time." For this is what the LORD Almighty, the God of Israel, says: "Houses, fields and vineyards will again be bought in the land."

Jeremiah 35:13

This is what the LORD Almighty, the God of Israel, says: "Go and tell the men of Judah and the people of Jerusalem, 'Will you not learn a lesson and obey my words?' " declares the LORD.

Jeremiah 35:17-19

Therefore, this is what the LORD God Almighty, the God of Israel, says: "Listen! I am going to bring on Judah and on everyone living in Jerusalem every disaster I pronounced against them. I spoke to them, but they did not listen; I called to them, but they did not answer."

Then Jeremiah said to the family of the Recabites, "This is what the LORD Almighty, the God of Israel, says: 'You have obeyed the command of your forefather Jonadab and have followed all his instructions and have done everything he ordered.' Therefore, this is what the LORD Almighty, the God of Israel, says: 'Jonadab son of Recab shall never fail to have a man to serve me.' "

Jeremiah 42:9, 10
He said to them, "This is what the LORD, the God of Israel, to whom you sent me to present your petition, says: 'If you stay in this land, I will build you up and not tear you down; I will plant you and not uproot you, for I am grieved over the disaster I have inflicted on you.' "

Ezekiel 9:3
Now the glory of the God of Israel went up from above the cherubim, where it had been, and moved to the threshold of the temple.

Ezekiel 10:18-20
Then the glory of the LORD departed from over the threshold of the temple and stopped above the cherubim. While I watched, the cherubim spread their wings and rose from the ground, and as they went, the wheels went with them. They stopped at the entrance to the east gate of the LORD's house, and the glory of the God of Israel was above them.

These were the living creatures I had seen beneath the God of Israel by the Kebar River, and I realized that they were cherubim.

Ezekiel 11:22, 23

Then the cherubim, with the wheels beside them, spread their wings, and the glory of the God of Israel was above them. The glory of the LORD went up from within the city [Jerusalem] and stopped above the mountain east of it [Mount of Olives].

Ezekiel 43:1, 2

Then the man brought me to the gate facing east, and I saw the glory of the God of Israel coming from the east. His voice was like the roar of rushing waters, and the land was radiant with his glory.

These scriptures are only seventy references to the God of Israel out of hundreds.

Chapter 3

God's Covenants with Abraham on Mt. Hermon for the Whole Land of Israel

The God of Israel makes a Covenant with Abraham on Mount Hermon for the Whole Land of Israel:

> **The Lord had said to Abram, "Leave your country, your people and your father's household and go to the land I will show you. I will make you into a great nation and I will bless you; I will make your name great, and you will be a blessing. I will bless those who bless you, and whoever curses you I will curse; and all peoples on earth will be blessed through you."**
>
> **So Abram left, as the Lord had told him; and Lot went with him. Abram was seventy-five years old when he set out from Haran. He took his wife Sarai, his nephew Lot, all the possessions they had accumulated and the people they had then acquired in Haran, and they set out for the land of Canaan, and they arrived there [probably Mount Hermon] (Genesis 12:1-5).**

The first place Abraham arrived at after departing from Haran, an ancient city in Iraq, was northern Israel. There it seems that he crossed over Mount Hermon. Jewish tradition says that God's covenant with Abraham in Genesis 15 took place on the heights of the Golan on top of Mount Hermon. Today, there is even a building there to commemorate it. I believe that the word of the Lord came to Abram in a vision and that the Lord made a covenant with him on Mount Hermon: "Do not be afraid, Abram. I am your shield, your very great reward" (Genesis 15:1). The covenant God of Israel is our shield. Also in Zechariah 12:8 the Lord said, "On that day the LORD will shield those who live in Jerusalem, so that the feeblest one will be like David, and the house of David will be like God, like the Angel of the LORD going before them."

Abraham thought Eliezer, the servant he brought from nearby Damascus, would be his heir, but God promised a son to come from his own body to be his heir.

> **He took him outside and said, "Look up at the heavens and count the stars—if indeed you can count them." Then he said to him, "So shall your offspring be."**
>
> **Abram believed the LORD, and he credited it to him as righteousness.**
>
> **He also said to him, "I am the LORD, who brought you out of Ur of the Chaldeans to give you this land to take possession of it" (Genesis 15:5-7).**

Then Abraham asks how he can know he will take possession of the land God promised him. God then made a covenant with Abraham.

> **So the LORD said to him, "Bring me a heifer, a goat and a ram, each three years old, along with a dove and a young pigeon."**
>
> **Abram brought all these to him, cut them in two and arranged the halves opposite each other; the birds, however, he did not cut in half. Then birds of prey came down on the carcasses, but Abram drove them away.**

26

As the sun was setting, Abram fell into a deep sleep, and a thick and dreadful darkness came over him. Then the LORD said to him, "Know for certain that your descendants will be strangers in a country not their own, and they will be enslaved and ill-treated four hundred years. But I will punish the nation they serve as slaves, and afterwards they will come out with great possessions. You, however, will go to your fathers in peace and be buried at a good old age. In the fourth generation your descendants will come back here, for the sin of the Amorites has not yet reached its full measure."

When the sun had set and darkness had fallen, a smoking brazier [oven] with a blazing torch appeared and passed between the pieces. On that day the LORD made a covenant with Abram and said, "To your descendants I give this land, from the river of Egypt to the great river, the Euphrates—the land of the Kenites, Kenizzites, Kadmonites, Hittites, Perizzites, Rephaites, Amorites, Canaanites, Girgashites and Jebusites (Genesis 15:9-21).

On that day God made a covenant with Abraham, recorded in Genesis 15, and said his descendants would receive the land from the river in Egypt to the great river of the Euphrates. Then Ishmael and Isaac were born who became two people groups. There has been a great conflict since that day between these two people groups, especially since the rebirth of Israel. It was meant to be a blessing to both—Jews and Arabs (Isaiah 19:23-25)—but the full fruit of salvation and reconciliation is yet to be fully realized.

Isaiah says Jerusalem's salvation will be like a blazing torch (62:1), like a blazing torch of reconciliation passing between Jews and Arabs.

Miraculously today, in these last days, God is committed to restoring these two groups into One in the Messiah. We will see those from the river of Egypt to the great river the Euphrates, Jews and Arabs of Egypt, Israel and Assyria worshiping God as a blessing in the midst of the earth.

> **In that day there will be a highway from Egypt to Assyria. The Assyrians will go to Egypt and the Egyptians to Assyria. The Egyptians and Assyrians will worship together. In that day Israel will be the third, along with Egypt and Assyria, a blessing on the earth. The LORD Almighty will bless them, saying, "Blessed be Egypt my people, Assyria my handiwork, and Israel my inheritance" (Isaiah 19:23-25).**

Genesis 1:27 says, "Let us make man in our image and likeness." Deuteronomy 6:4 says, "Hear O Israel: the LORD our God, the LORD is one." God is one as Mount Hermon is one mountain. Mount Hermon has three peaks: one in Israel, one in Lebanon, and one in Syria. This mountain is divided just as Jews and Arabs in these nations are divided. Arabs and Jews from all of these areas will become one. Psalm 133 says:

> **How good and pleasant it is when brothers live together in unity! It is like precious oil poured on the head, running down on the beard, [from the Covenant God of Israel in Heaven] running down on Aaron's beard, down upon the collar of his robes. It is as if the dew of Hermon were falling on the peaks of Mt. Zion.**

IT IS AS IF THE DEW OF HERMON WERE FALLING ON THE PEAKS OF MOUNT ZION. This will happen from all the peaks

28

of Hermon to the heartland of Israel, Samaria and Judea—Shechem, Beth El, Hebron, and Jerusalem—to the skirts of the garments of Israel in Eilat. For there the Lord bestows His blessings, even life forevermore. It was also on Mount Hermon, believed by some to be the Mount of Transfiguration, that Peter said, "You are the Christ, Son of the living God" and the place where Peter, James and John, wanted to build three tabernacles in Ceasarea Philippi. Their desire to build three tabernacles on Mount Hermon and Mount Hermon's three peaks points to the fact that the tabernacle of God—Father, Son, and Holy Spirit—is with man.

> **Abram traveled [from Mount Hermon in the Golan] through the land as far as the site of the great tree of Moreh in Shechem. At that time the Canaanites were in the land, The LORD appeared to Abram and said, "To your offspring I will give you this land." So he built an altar there to the LORD, who had appeared to him (Genesis 12:6,7).**

After God made a covenant with Abraham, God called forth Abraham's two sons, Ishmael and Isaac. For the next four thousand years there has been conflict rooted in enmity between these two brothers. Praise God, we are in the days of restoration. Abraham is not only the father of Isaac and Ishmael, but Abraham is the father of every believer on the planet. All Christian believers, including Arabs, are children of Abraham by faith.

The Lord Commands Joshua to Fulfill His Covenant by Possessing the Whole Land

> **After the death of Moses the servant of the LORD, the LORD said to Joshua son of Nun, Moses' assistant: " Moses my servant is dead. Now then, you and all these people, get**

ready to cross the Jordan River into the land I am about to give to them—to the Israelites. I will give you every place where you set your foot, as I promised Moses. Your territory will extend from the desert to Lebanon, and from the great river, the Euphrates—all the Hittite country—to the Great Sea on the west. Noone will be able to stand up against you all the days of your life. As I was with Moses, so I will be with you; I will never leave you nor forsake you.

"Be strong and courageous, because you will lead these people to inherit the land I swore to their forefathers to give them. Be strong and very courageous. Be careful to obey all the law my servant Moses gave you; do not turn from it to the right or to the left, that you may be successful wherever you go. Do not let this Book of the Law depart from your mouth; meditate on it day and night, so that you may be careful to do everything written in it. Then you will be prosperous and successful. Have I not commanded you? Be strong and courageous. Do not be terrified; do not be discouraged, for the LORD your God will be with you wherever you go."

So Joshua ordered the officers of the people: "Go through the camp and tell the people: 'Get your supplies ready. Three days from now you will cross the Jordan here to get in and take possession of the land the LORD your God is giving you for your own' " (Joshua 1:1-11).

God is speaking this word again today to Jews in the land as he did four thousand years ago. He is speaking this word today to Arab-Christians and Christians worldwide to stand with the God of Israel and His covenants with the land to be fully possessed both naturally and spiritually.

PART II

Restoring the Four Covenantal Altars- The Foundations and Pillars of the House of Israel

I believe we are coming full circle in history, returning to the roots in Jerusalem and Israel. The greatest battles in Israel today, which affect all of the Middle East and the whole world, are in the places where Abraham built altars to God and where God made covenants with His people. In Shechem (Nablus), Beth El (Ramallah), Hebron (Kiryat Arba), and Mt. Moriah (Jerusalem), where Abraham, Jacob and David built the four altars and pillars to the Lord, here God made covenants with them and their offspring.

After the seriously failed attempt of the Oslo Accords and the Road Map of the Nations, Israel seems to not have learned from that tragic mistake. Today plans are again being made to try to give this land, the heartland of Israel and the places of God's covenant with Israel, for a Palestinian Islamic State. Bible-believing Jews and Christians need to rise in faith together to stand with God's covenant to possess and restore the altars, foundations, and pillars in Israel's heartland.

Chapter 4

The Shechem Covenantal Promise Altar

The first altar Abraham built was in Shechem. When Abraham arrived in Shechem the Lord appeared to him and said, **"To your offspring I will give this land"** (Genesis 12:7). There he built his first altar. When he built the first altar to the Lord in Shechem, God said He would give him the land. When God promises something to someone He makes a covenant with them. He made a covenant with Abraham saying, **"To your offspring I will give this land."**

Not only did God give the land to Abraham's offspring in Shechem, but also to Jacob:

> **After Jacob came from Paddan Aram, he arrived safely at the city of Shechem in Canaan and camped within sight of the city. For a hundred pieces of silver, he bought from the sons of Hamor, the father of Shechem, the plot of ground where he pitched his tent. There he set up an altar and called it El Elohe Israel [lit. God the God of Israel] (Genesis 33:18).**

In Shechem, Jacob formally acknowledged the God of his father as his God. Hallelujah! God brought Jacob back to the same place where God made a covenant with Abraham and where Abraham built an altar. Because God made a covenant with Abraham first, Jacob could see what God did in regard to its establishment, return to that place and renew the covenant. There, Jacob bought land and, like his forefather, built an altar unto the Lord. Because

Jacob recognized the seriousness of the commitment of God to make covenants with Israel in this place, he not only built an altar, but also bought the piece of land and dug a well.

As described in Genesis 37, we know that near Shechem, where the covenants were made, his brothers sold Joseph into slavery into Egypt where the Jews lived for four hundred years. Joshua 24:32 says that after coming out of Egypt four hundred years later:

> **Joseph's bones, which the Israelites had brought up from Egypt, were buried [back] at Shechem in the tract of land that Jacob bought for a hundred pieces of silver from the sons of Hamor, the father of Shechem. This became the inheritance of Joseph's descendants.**

Also near Shechem, in the hill country of Ephraim, God gave Joshua, one of Joseph's descendants, his inheritance—Timnath Serah—a city in Samaria (Joshua 20:49, 50).

Joshua's Altar in Shechem

Four hundred years after Joseph was sold into slavery in Egypt, as Abraham saw would happen in his vision in Genesis 15, Joshua led the Israelites into the land promised as an oath to Abraham, Isaac, Jacob, and their descendants as an inheritance. When Joshua came to Shechem, he built an altar to the Lord as Moses commanded in Deuteronomy 27:

> **Then Joshua built on Mount Ebal an altar to the LORD, the God of Israel, as Moses the servant of the LORD had commanded the Israelites. He built it according to what is written in the Book**

34

of the Law of Moses—an altar of uncut stones, on which no iron tool had been used. On it they offered to the LORD burnt offerings and sacrificed fellowship offerings. There, in the presence of the Israelites, Joshua copied on stones the law of Moses, which he had written. All Israel, aliens and citizens alike, with their elders, officials and judges, were standing on both sides of the ark of the covenant of the LORD, facing whose who carried it—the priests, who were Levites. Half of the people stood in front of Mount Gerizim and half of them in front of Mount Ebal [with the city of Shechem between the two mountains], as Moses the servant of the LORD had formerly commanded when he gave instruction to bless the people of Israel.

Afterwards, Joshua read all the words of the law—the blessings and the curses—just as it is written in the Book of the Law. There was not a word of all that Moses had commanded that Joshua did not read to the whole assembly of Israel, including the women and children, and the aliens who lived among them (Joshua 8:30-35).

The Covenant with God and with the Land Renewed at Shechem

After Joshua and the armies of Israel took the land, the covenant God made with Abraham and Jacob, His promise of the land to Israel, was renewed in Shechem. Shechem is the place where God promised the land to Abraham, the place where Jacob bought land and dug a well, and the place where altars were built. It is a foundation in Israel's heartland and a pillar of the house of Israel.

Then Joshua assembled all the tribes of Israel at Shechem. He summoned the elders, leaders, judges and officials of Israel, and they presented themselves before God.

Joshua said to all the people, "This is what the LORD, the God of Israel, says: 'Long ago your forefathers, including Terah the father of Abraham and Nahor, lived beyond the River and worshiped other gods. But I took your father Abraham from the land beyond the River and led him throughout Canaan and gave him many descendants. I gave him Isaac, and to Isaac I gave Jacob and Esau. I assigned the hill country of Seir to Esau, but Jacob and his sons went down to Egypt.

"'Then I sent Moses and Aaron, and I afflicted the Egyptians by what I did there, and I brought you out. When I brought your fathers out of Egypt, you came to the sea, and the Egyptians pursued them with chariots and horsemen as far as the Red Sea. But they cried to the LORD for help, and he put darkness between you and the Egyptians; he brought the sea over them and covered them. You saw with your own eyes what I did to the Egyptians. Then you lived in the desert for a long time.

"'I brought you to the land of the Amorites who lived east of the Jordan. They fought against you, but I gave them into your hands. I destroyed them from before you, and you took possession of their land. When Balak son of Zippor, the king of Moab, prepared to fight against Israel, he sent for Balaam son of Beor to put a curse on you. But I would not listen to Balaam, so he blessed you again and again, and I delivered you out of his hand.

"'Then you crossed the Jordan and came to Jericho. The citizens of Jericho fought against you, as did also the Amorites, Perizzites, Canaanites, Hittites, Girgashites, Hivites and Jebusites, but I gave them into your hands. I sent the hornet ahead of you, which drove them out before you—also the two Amorite kings. You did not do it with your own sword and bow. So I gave you a land on which you did not toil and cities you did not build; and you live in them and eat from vineyards and olive groves that you did not plant.'

"Now fear the LORD and serve him with all faithfulness. Throw away the gods your forefathers worshipped beyond the River and in Egypt, and serve the LORD. But if serving the LORD seem undesirable to you, then choose for yourselves this day whom you will serve, whether the gods your forefathers served before you beyond the River, or the gods of the Amorites, in whose land you are living. But as for me and my household, we will serve the LORD."

Then the people answered, "Far be it from us to forsake the LORD and serve other gods! It was the LORD our God himself who brought us and our fathers up out of the land of Egypt, from the land of slavery, and performed those great signs before our eyes. He protected us on our entire journey and among all the nations through which we traveled. And the LORD drove out before us all the nations, including the Amorites, who lived in the land. We too will serve the LORD, because he is our God."

Joshua said to the people, "You are not able to serve the LORD. He is a holy God; he is a jealous God. He will not forgive your rebellion and your sins. If you forsake the LORD and serve foreign gods, he will turn and bring disaster on you and make an end of you, after he has been good to you."

But the people said to Joshua, "No! We will serve the LORD."

Then Joshua said, "You are witnesses against yourselves that you have chosen to serve the LORD."

"Yes, we are witnesses," they replied.

"Now then," said Joshua, 'throw away the foreign gods that are among you and yield your hearts to the LORD, the God of Israel."

And the people said to Joshua, "We will serve the LORD our God and obey him."

On that day Joshua made a covenant for the people, and there at Shechem he drew up for them decrees and laws. And Joshua recorded these things in the Book of the Law of God. Then he took a large stone and set it up there under the oak near the holy place of the LORD.

"See!" he said to all the people. "This stone will be a witness against us. It has heard all the words the LORD has said to us. It will be a witness against you if you are untrue to your God" (Joshua 24:1-27).

It is time again for all Jews to renew the covenant with God and the land in Shechem. During Passover 2002 five Jews were murdered in Elon Moreh, the Jewish neighborhood of Shechem. Since October 2002 Jews were forbidden by Israeli law to visit Joseph's tomb. Four months later, in February 2003, Joseph's tomb was destroyed by Muslim terrorists in Shechem trying to drive the Jewish people from these foundational places of covenant. Few Jews or Christians reacted or protested. If Jews are the children of Abraham and Christians are children of Abraham by faith, then why do they allow the places of the foundations of our faith to be destroyed? Christians do not allow the Holy Sepulchre or the Garden Tomb to be destroyed, nor do Muslims allow Mecca or the Dome of the Rock to be destroyed. Why do the Jews allow the place where land was first promised to them and the place of the first covenant altar, the land that Jacob purchased and where Joseph's Tomb is, to be destroyed and confiscated?

Today at the beginning of the twenty-first century, this covenant needs to be again renewed in Shechem by Jews in the land of Israel and supported by Bible-believing Arab-Christians and Christians worldwide.

The Ministry of Jesus in Shechem

In John 4, when Jesus ministered to the Samaritan woman at Jacob's well, which is in Shechem on the ground Jacob purchased and near where Joseph's bones were buried, Jesus asked her for a drink from the well and told her that she should receive living water, the Holy Spirit.

> **She asked, "Are you greater than our father Jacob, who gave us the well and drank from it himself, as did also his sons and his flocks and herds."**
> **Jesus answered, "Everyone who drinks this water will be thirsty again, but whoever drinks the water I give him will never thirst. Indeed, the water I give him will become in him a spring of water welling up to eternal life" (John 4:12-14).**

Jesus told her:

"You Samaritans worship what you do not know; we [Jews] worship what we do know, for salvation is from the Jews. Yet a time is coming and has now come when the true worshipers will worship the Father in spirit and in truth, for they are the kind of worshipers the Father seeks" **(John 4:22,23).**

This story of Jesus with the Samaritan woman in Shechem two thousand years ago is exactly what God wants to do there again. God purposes to rebuild the altars and to redig the wells that bring Jews and Arabs in Shechem/Elon Moreh to worship the God of Israel together in spirit and truth. It is the foundation of Egypt, Israel, and Assyria worshiping Him together as a blessing in the midst of the earth (Isaiah 19:23-25). Today, Arabs from Shechem are believing in Messiah, embracing the God of Israel, the Jewish people, and God's covenants with the heartland of Israel first made in Shechem preparing the way for God's peace plan. Only as Jews and Arabs together fully embrace the Holy Spirit and the full truth in the Bible about His covenants will His peace plan prevail. Then they can fully worship the God of Israel together in Spirit and in Truth as reconciled and restored sons of Abraham and a blessing in the midst of the earth.

An Iraqi Christian who led two Shechemites to trust in the God of Israel and His Abrahamic Covenant shares his testimony:

I was born in Iraq, to a family of nine children. At school in Iraq, we were taught to hate the Jews and the Zionist movement. We were brain-washed with all kinds of myths and anti-Semitic teachings. Faith in God and my relationship with Jesus is the way I came to be interested in the Middle East situation.

For an Arab to love a Jew, he must have a revelation from God. Only a profound encounter with the love of God can melt the hardened heart of an Arab to open his heart to the Jews. The love that came into my heart through Jesus is pure and unconditional for everyone alike—Jews and Arabs, black or white. When I received the Lord Jesus, my prayer was, "Here I am Lord, what do you want me to do?" The consequence of that prayer is that six times He led me into this blessed land [of Israel] as a messenger of peace. He brought an Iraqi, their "enemy" in the conflict saga, to tell the Jews that their God is the true God. I come to Israel to tell the Jews I love their God and I love them too. I want to be an instrument in God's hand to open the chains of hate and allow the river of love to flow out of Iraq into Israel.

My congregation consists of Palestinians, Lebanese, Syrians, and Iraqis. We all love Israel and we pray every day for the peace of Jerusalem and for reconciliation between Arabs and Jews. We sing Hebrew and Arabic songs and we openly share our faith in the God of Israel and that our foundation entirely rest in biblical teaching. In my lifetime I want to see Isaiah 19:23-25 come to pass.

Near Shechem, Ron Nachman is the mayor of Ariel, the second largest city in Judea and Samaria next to Ma'ale Adumim. Mayor Nachman, who is a strong believer in the God of Israel and a friend to Christians, has opened his office on a weekly basis for Christians to visit and pray to the God of Israel for Ariel, Judea and Samaria. This is another strong sign of reconciliation and solidarity between Christians and Jewish people regarding God's covenants and His land.

Chapter 5

The Beth El Covenantal Promise Altar

From there [Shechem] he [Abram] went on towards the hills east of Bethel and pitched his tent, with Bethel on the west and Ai on the east. There he built an altar to the LORD and he called on the name of the LORD (Genesis 12:8).

The next place Abraham came to after building the altar in Shechem is Beth El. There he built another altar unto the Lord. Shechem and Beth El are places of the Lord's foundational covenants made with Israel, the Jewish people.

After building the first two altars, Abraham set out for the Negev and went down to Egypt, to Africa. I don't think he went all the way down to South Africa, but he did go to Africa. I believe there is a special place for the African nations because Egypt is the place for prophetic birthing. Abraham comes out of Egypt, the children of Israel were called out of Egypt, and Messiah was called out of Egypt. God says the highway in the last days will come from Egypt through Israel to Assyria (Isaiah 19:23-25). Joseph was first revealed to his brothers in Egypt. Bethlehem, the city of David and Jesus, is even located in this gateway. It is a gateway of prophetic birthing.

After Abraham came out of Egypt he returned to the place where he built the altar to the Lord in Beth El. While in Beth El, God spoke to Abraham:

The LORD said to Abram after Lot had departed from him, "Lift up your eyes from where

you are [Beth El] and look north and south, east and west. All the land that you see I will give to you and your offspring for ever. I will make your offspring like the dust of the earth, so that if anyone could count the dust, then your offspring could be counted. Go, walk through the length and breadth of the land, for I am giving it to you" (Genesis 13:14-17).

When I was in today's Beth El community over Passover 2003, one of the twenty-five year residents living there told me what he has seen from Beth El. He said that he has seen snow on Mt. Hermon to the north; Jerusalem, Gaza and the mountains of Hebron to the south; the mountains of Jordan to the east; and the Mediterranean Sea and Tel Aviv to the west. He, like Abraham, saw the land promised by the God of Israel from Beth El.

Abraham was not the only one who built an altar to the Lord in Beth El:

Jacob left Beersheba and set out for Haran. When he reached a certain place, he stopped for the night because the sun had set. Taking one of the stones there, he put it under his head and lay down to sleep. He had a dream in which he saw a stairway resting on the earth, with its top reaching to heaven, and the angels of God were ascending and descending on it. There above it stood the LORD, and he said: "I am the LORD, the God of your father Abraham and the God of Isaac. I will give you and your descendants the land on which you are lying. Your descendants will be like the dust of the earth, and you will spread out to the west and to the east, to the north and to the south. All the peoples on earth will be blessed through

you and your offspring. I am with you and will watch over you wherever you go, and I will bring you back to this land. I will not leave you until I have done what I have promised you."

When Jacob awoke from his sleep, he thought, "Surely the LORD is in this place, and I was not aware of it." He was afraid and said, "How awesome is this place! This is none other than the house of God [Beth El]; this is the gate of heaven" (Genesis 28:10-17).

Jacob returned to Beth El, because he wanted to enter into the covenants of his father. When God makes covenants with people, they want to return to those places of covenant.

Early the next morning Jacob took the stone he had placed under his head and he set it up as a pillar and poured oil on top of it. He called that place Beth El [House of God], though the city used to be called Luz.

Then Jacob made a vow, saying, "If God will be with me and will watch over me on this journey I am taking and will give me food to eat and clothes to wear so that I return safely to my father's house, then the LORD will be my God and this stone that I have set up as a pillar will be God's house, and of all that you give me I will give you a tenth" (Genesis 28:18-22).

God was with Abraham in Beth El and brought Jacob back and opened the heavens and opened His covenants from the heavens, on earth with Jacob. I believe where this happened was in the heart of the garden of Eden, which was between the Nile River and the Euphrates River and that in this region God will fulfill Isaiah

45

19: **"The Egyptians and the Assyrians will worship together. In that day Israel will be the third, along with Egypt and Assyria, a blessing on the earth."**

Jacob returned to Beth El again in Genesis 35. There in Beth El, the place of making covenants and setting up pillars, God changed Jacob's name to Israel.

> **God said to him, "Your name is Jacob, but you will no longer be called Jacob; your name will be Israel." So He named him Israel.**
>
> **And God said to him, "I am God Almighty; be fruitful and increase in number. A nation and a community of nations will come from you, and kings will come from your body. The land I gave to Abraham and Isaac I also give to you, and I will give this land to your descendants after you" (Genesis 35:10-12).**

Beth El is the place where Israel was conceived (Genesis 12 & 28), born (Genesis 35), and the name of Jacob changed to Israel.

Passover in Beth El

For Passover 2002, Yossi Kapach, a Yemenite orthodox Jew invited me to come to Beth El. He had previously come to the *All Americas Convocation* where we had gathered sixty-two survivors of the S/S St. Louis and their spouses together with Christians from all over the Americas. The Christians repented to the Jews for rejecting this ship filled with Jewish people from landing in Cuba and/or the shores of South Florida and sending them back to die in the Holocaust. This orthodox Jew brought messages of greetings to the convocation from the Prime Minister of Israel and the Mayor of Jerusalem. He invited us to his home in Beth El.

46

In Beth El that Passover, we saw twelve thousand soldiers and over a thousand tanks posted at the gates of the city. Yasser Arafat's headquarters are one kilometer from Beth El in Ramallah. All of a sudden, my eyes began to open more. I began to discern why Arafat is not in Gaza, the center of his people:

After Solomon sinned, his kingdom split. Jeroboam, in rebellion with the Northern Kingdom of Israel, built an altar to Baal and a golden calf in Beth El (I Kings 12:25-13:10). Hosea and Amos spoke of this as the worst idolatry in Israel (Hosea 4:15; 5: 8; 10:8; Amos 4:4; 5:5). Today, Arafat and Islam are trying to rebuild the altar of Baal in Ramallah (Beth El). The Palestinian Authority even has Baal on its postage stamp! There must be identificational repentance by believers for these sins both from the Jewish and Arab side in these days as in Daniel 9:4&5. Daniel prayed, **"We have sinned and done wrong. We have been wicked and have rebelled; we have turned away from your commands and laws."** I believe Israel must renounce and repent of Baal worship in Beth El and the Palestinian Arab-Christians must also repent before the land of Israel and Jewish and Arab people will be restored and united. In Tayibe, a neighboring village to Beth El, some Arab-Christians believe in the God of Israel to fully restore the land and people in the Jewish Messiah.

For twelve years we have come to these four places— Shechem, Beth El, Hebron, Jerusalem—to build altars and stand with God's covenants and God's covenant people. Since Passover 2002 my eyes were opened in a fuller way, and I began to see the greater significance of the places where Abraham, Isaac, and Jacob (whose name was changed to Israel) built altars. I began to realize what the enemies of Israel are trying to do. They are trying to destroy the foundations, knock down the pillars of the house of Israel, and cause the Jewish people to break covenants with their God in the very places where God made covenants with His people.

Terrorists and all who do not understand God's covenants are trying to drive the Jewish people out of this land (from what they

47

call settlements) promised to them by God. That is what terrorism in Israel is all about, trying to uproot God's covenant people and lay the foundations of Islam in the places where God made covenants with His people.

All replacement theologies and ideologies are born out of rebellion against the Covenant God of Israel and the Abrahamic covenants. Those who deny God's just choice of Isaac and Jacob, whose name was changed to Israel, and say that God chose Ishmael or other replacements instead of Isaac are enemies of peace. This is because they worship another god, a moon god, not the Covenant God of Israel. They teach that the whole world, especially the heartland of Israel, should submit to another god. It is not a matter of giving the Palestinian people land to live on. It is not as in South Africa where the human rights issue of land for people to live on is the problem. No! In Israel, we are dealing with something that has to do with the kingdoms of darkness against the kingdom of our Lord and Messiah. WE ARE DEALING WITH COVENANTS. Those in the nations need to understand that we are dealing with the covenants of the God of Israel and His land and His people.

The God of Israel Blessing the Arabs
BIBLICAL HIGHWAY ROAD MAP OF RECONCILIATION

I love the Arab people. Both where I live in Jerusalem and all over the Middle East, I have very close friendships with many Arabs whom I treasure as friends and who are standing in solidarity with God's covenants and covenant people. Not only the Jews, but Arabs too are natural children of Abraham. Ishmael was circumcised with Abraham and God promised many blessings for him.

And Abraham said to God, "If only Ishmael might live under your blessing!"

48

To be fully blessed, he must properly relate to God's Abrahamic Covenants with Jacob-Israel in regard to the land and salvation. The blessing is a sign that he also is to be included in the covenant with Jacob-Israel if he does not rebel, but receives the covenant!

> **Then God said, "And as for Ishmael, I have heard you: I will surely bless him; I will make him fruitful and will greatly increase his numbers. He will be a father of twelve nations. He will be the father of twelve rulers, and I will make him into a great nation" (Genesis 17:18, 20, 21).**

Most Arabs are yet to come into the fullness of their blessing. The God of Israel is a covenant-keeping God. He has a covenant with Ishmael to bring a blessing upon him. But the covenants of God are in terms of the seed of redemption. The covenants of God are in terms of this land being passed down through the descendants of Jacob, through Israel. The only way the God of Israel is going to fully bless the Arab people is if they recognize the covenants God made with Israel, recognize God's fullest blessings upon themselves through Jacob-Israel, and choose to bless Israel. Then, they will be fully blessed.

Today, I see Arabs beginning to bless Israel and stand with God's purposes for Israel. God is blessing them. Anyone who blesses God will be blessed. God will even make them a blessing together, not just the Jews a blessing by themselves. Some people say all the Arabs can go to hell, and God will only bless the Jews. No! God is going to bring Egypt, Israel, and Assyria together and bless them together. Together they are going to worship God. Together they are going to be a blessing in the midst of the earth.

> **In that day there will be a highway from Egypt to Assyria. The Assyrians will go to Egypt**

and the Egyptians to Assyria. The Egyptians and Assyrians will worship together. In that day Israel will be the third, along with Egypt and Assyria, a blessing on the earth. The LORD Almighty will bless them, saying, "Blessed be Egypt my people, Assyria my handiwork, and Israel my inheritance" (Isaiah 19:23-25).

All over the world, reports are made about the Occupied Territories. Reports include what people call the "West Bank" and the proposal of a Palestinian State.

THE FOUR PLACES WHERE ABRAHAM BUILT ALTARS ARE IN THE HEART OF THESE AREAS, THE VERY CENTER OF ISRAEL....

THE VERY CENTER OF THE LAND THAT IS SAID SHOULD BE AN ISLAMIC PALESTINIAN STATE BY THOSE WHO DO NOT BELIEVE IN THE GOD OF ISRAEL AND HIS COVENANTS....

THE VERY CENTER OF THE LAND ISLAM CALLS "OCCUPIED TERRITORY"....

THE VERY CENTER OF THE LAND BIBLICALLY CALLED JUDEA AND SAMARIA...

Some people think all the Arabs should be taken out of those places and only the Jews should live there. I believe what God wants to do is for Bible-believing Arab-Christians and Christians in the nations to stand with the Jewish people who are standing in these areas, hold up their arms and support them, standing for the covenants of God.

We must support them first of all naturally, because the Bible says, first the natural than the spiritual. We must also ask God to pour out His protection and Spirit upon His people, the Jewish people, so that they will recognize the God of Israel. We need to stand in solidarity with His people and God's covenants made with them—that they will not be driven out of their land, but stay there and worship God in these places. God says in Ezekiel 36 that He is going to fill the hills of Judea and Samaria with His people.

We should not pray that the Arabs be driven out of these places. God wants the Arabs to stay there and recognize and enter into God's covenants and be reconciled with the Jews as a blessing on the earth, worshiping Him together unless they are unwilling, in which case they may have to leave. If God says He is going to do this all over the Middle East, from Egypt, Israel and Assyria, then it needs to be done first and foremost in the very places where God's Abrahamic covenants were made.

Beth El is the place where God said to Abraham, "Your heirs are going to be blessed."

God said, in this place He will not only bless the Jews, but He also said that He will bless all the nations. Beth El is the place where God said to Abraham, "Your heirs are going to be blessed." Christians are the offspring of Abraham by faith coming into the promise through Messiah. He said the same thing to the Arabs. He said He wants to bless them from Beth El.

Mokhtar, from Tunisia, who now believes in the God of Israel, repented at the synagogue in Beth El because of his past hatred of the Jews and blessed them. He says, "When I was born-again by reading the Torah, I came to repent of my wrong attitude towards Torah, the Jews, and my thoughts about Israel." On *Yom Kippur*, he realized that the Church must repent of and be cleansed of replacement theology, a way of interpreting scriptures that completely replaces the natural Israel with a spiritual Christian Church.

The blindness needs to come off the Arab people so that they can enter into the promises of Abraham by faith as mentioned in this book and in the Bible. We need to pray that God will remove the blindness and that they will enter into the covenants God made with Israel through Abraham, Isaac, and Jacob. I believe this. Although it seems ridiculous and impossible in the natural, even the most ridiculous thing in the world, we are confident that with the God of Israel all things are possible. This will happen because the Bible tells me so!

I believe that at the foundation of fulfilling Isaiah 19 and reconciling Jews and Arabs is Egypt, Israel and Assyria worshiping together as a blessing on the earth in the places of God's foundational covenants. Unless restoration happens regarding the covenants of the God of Israel in the heartland of Israel, how is it going to be released as a blessing throughout Egypt, Israel, Assyria, and the earth? If the foundations are destroyed, how can the righteous stand? If the foundation of God's covenanted places and the pillars of Israel are destroyed, how are we going to see Isaiah 19 fulfilled? If you take down the pillars and foundations of the House of Israel, disregarding the covenants of the God of Israel, then how can Israel stand and come into her full restoration and destiny in Messiah?

If the foundation of God's covenanted places and the pillars of Israel are destroyed, how are we going to see Isaiah 19 fulfilled?

It is no accident that God wants to move in these places last. In this age of restoration, He is moving from the ends of the earth, through the gateways back to the Middle East, back to Israel, through Judea and Samaria, into Jerusalem. We are moving in restoration from the ends of the earth back to the original places of God's covenants.

Today, when we go to these places of covenant and pray that the God of Israel will fully bless the natural descendants of Abraham, we pray not just for Jews, but also for Arabs. We pray for the restoration of the roots of our faith of all who are children of Abraham, both natural and spiritual children. God is a miracle-working God.

At Passover 2003 with twenty-five Bible-believing Christians, we were invited again back to Beth El, this time by the former Minister of Tourism, Rabbi Benny Elon (who spoke with our group and recognizes Bible-believing Christians as Israel's best friend), to stand with them in prayer for the Jewish community of Beth El to remain a part of Israel. I believe that in the coming years we are going to see the God of the Breakthrough cause many breakthroughs. There may be many struggles and many challenges, but the God of Israel is the God of restoration. Amen!

Occupy Until I Come: Fulfilling Isaiah 19

People talk about all kinds of things happening. I don't know when some prophecies in the Bible will be fulfilled, but the scriptures say we should occupy until He comes. We know the covenant God of Israel will fulfill his covenantal promises with the land and with the people of Isaiah 19 from the Nile to the Euphrates.

I believe for the fullness. Although we do not know when Isaiah 19 is going to be fulfilled, I know it will be fulfilled. Some people say it is going to be fulfilled later. Some people say it is going to be fulfilled now. I don't know when its going to be fulfilled, but let's press on and believe God for the fullness of what He wills to be fulfilled in our days.

The Christian community is called to occupy until Messiah comes. I would hate to give up and say, this is too difficult and be sitting back in my little prayer room or in a cave or on the beach somewhere while all along Isaiah 19 is being fulfilled before the Messiah comes. I would be sitting there like an idiot, not even involved in the process. None of us have the last word when He will come. But the Lord says to occupy until I come. As long as we are alive we want to believe God for the fullness of His Word that can be fulfilled in our times, to be fulfilled. Let's believe that whatever can be fulfilled will be fulfilled before Messiah comes knowing that it will be completely fulfilled when he comes.

It is already beginning to happen. Today, there are believers in every Arab nation. When we started praying ten years ago in our first Convocation, there were no believers in four Arab nations. In our past gatherings in Cyprus, we have had believers from every Arab nation represented to worship the covenant God of Israel. We can say there are at least cell groups in every Arab nation. First fruits have already come forth!

That first fruits that come forth are a sign that the fullness is coming. I believe in God that much will be fulfilled before Messiah comes. God is a God of fullness. Therefore He does not want us to shrink back, but to press forward and believe Him for the fullness of the salvation of Egypt, Israel, and Assyria worshiping God as a blessing in the midst of the earth.

On September 29, 2000, when the *Intifada* began in Israel, many of you were attending the *All Nations Convocation Jerusalem* praying in the gap for those situations. That made the difference and makes a difference today. I believe that many things intended by the enemy in these days will be averted. We need to stand in the gap and believe God for fullness. Do not shrink back, but press forward. We do not know when the fullness will come, but God said, **occupy until I come**.

In Genesis 35:9,10 it says:

> **After Jacob returned from Paddan Aram,
> God appeared to him again and blessed him. God
> said to him, 'Your name is Jacob, but you will no
> longer be called Jacob; your name will be Israel.'
> So He named him Israel.**

Jacob had a divine encounter with the God of Israel. He connected with heaven in Beth El, the Gate of Heaven. He had a similar experience as Abraham did with Melchizedek and was never the same. He saw angels ascending and descending a ladder. I believe the reason he did not buy the land in Beth El is because his

54

encounter with the God of Israel covenanted all of Israel with the God of Israel in Heaven in such a way that it opened up the way for land to be purchased in Shechem, Hebron, and Jerusalem by Jacob, Abraham, and David as pillars for the House of Israel.

In Beth El, Jacob was named Israel. This is a pillar for the whole House of Israel and a foundation of the House of God, also called the house of prayer for all nations. Yet the enemies of Israel and even many Jews who do not believe in the God of Israel and His covenants say all Jews should leave the places of covenant—Shechem, Beth El, Hebron, Jerusalem. That is what the nations of the world are demanding. That is what the Muslims are demanding. Even many Jews including some orthodox and nominal Christians who do not understand the scriptures in this book are demanding this as well. They say the only way there can be peace is when the Jews leave the places of covenants that the God of Israel made with them.

In light of this, I believe the Oslo Peace Accord and the Road Map are false peace accords. They said the only way for peace is to remove the Jewish people from the places of covenant and let the enemies of the Covenant God of Israel take over the foundations. There is no way there will be true *shalom/salaam* except through the Prince of Peace (Isaiah 9:6). The prophet Isaiah sheds light on the first Oslo agreement (known as the Declaration of Principles), which was signed on the White House lawn on September 13, 1993—the 27th day of Ellul on the Hebrew Calendar. Taking the vantage-point of one day after the agreement—September 14, or Ellul 28—one may look to Isaiah 28:14 and the scriptures that follow it.

Therefore hear the word of the LORD, you scoffers who rule this people in Jerusalem. You boast, "We have entered into a covenant with death, with the grave we have made an agreement. When an overwhelming scourge sweeps by it cannot touch us, for we have made a lie our refuge and falsehood our hiding-place."

55

So this is what the Sovereign LORD says: "See, I lay a stone in Zion, a tested stone, a precious cornerstone for a sure foundation; the one who trusts will never be dismayed. Your covenant with death will be annulled; your agreement with the grave will not stand" (Isaiah 28:14-16, 18).

The only way there is going to be real *shalom/salaam* in Israel before Messiah's coming is if the Jews and the Arabs in these places both recognize and trust in the God of Israel and the Bible, and then reconcile to each other in Him. The Arabs must recognize that God made covenants with the land of Israel and with the Jewish people and they must accept them. The Jews must recognize not only the covenants of God with the land of Israel and the Jewish people, but also that God said they should treat all the aliens in the land, the Arabs, who are ready to live at peace with them, who trust in the God of Israel, and who reject the lie of replacement theologies and ideologies, as native-born Israelis. They should treat them as their own flesh and blood and allow them to settle in the land as it says in Ezekiel 47:21-23:

"You are to distribute this land among yourselves according to the tribes of Israel. You are to allot it as an inheritance for yourselves and for the aliens [Arabs] who have settled among you and who have children. You are to consider them as native-born Israelites; along with you they are to be allotted an inheritance among the tribes of Israel. In whatever tribe the alien settles, there you are to give him his inheritance," declares the Sovereign LORD.

Chapter 6

The Hebron Covenantal Promise Altar

After Abraham left Beth El he went to Hebron, near the trees of Mamre, where he built his third altar.

> **The LORD said to Abram after Lot had departed from him, "Lift up your eyes from where you are and look north and south, east and west. All the land that you see I will give to you and your offspring for ever. I will make your offspring like the dust of the earth, so that if anyone could count the dust, then your offspring could be counted. Go, walk through the length and breadth of the land, for I am giving it to you."**
>
> **So Abram moved his tents and went to live near the great trees of Mamre at Hebron, where he built an altar to the LORD (Genesis 13:14-18).**

In Hebron, Abraham bought land—the field, cave, and all the trees on the field at Machpelah—to posses as a burial site for his wife and descendants. This land became a legal possession and inheritance in the presence of all the Hittites. The King of the Hittites could not collect taxes unless the entire field including all of its trees were purchased.

> **So Ephron's field in Machpelah near Mamre—both the field and the cave in it, and all the trees within the borders of the field—was**

legally made over to Abraham as his property in the presence of all the Hittites who had come to the gate of the city. Afterwards Abraham buried his wife Sarah in the cave in the field of Machpelah near Mamre [which is at Hebron] in the land of Canaan. So the field and the cave in it were legally made over to Abraham by the Hittites as a burial site (Genesis 23:17-20).

The place where Abraham built his third altar, Hebron, is a very significant city. It represents fatherhood and means friendship. Hebron is the home of the fathers. It is the place where Abraham, Isaac, and Jacob lived and were buried. Jewish tradition says that even Adam and Eve were buried in Hebron. The word of the Lord to Isaiah said:

Listen to me, you who pursue righteousness and who seek the LORD; look to the rock from which you were cut and to the quarry from which you were hewn; look to Abraham, your father, and to Sarah, who gave you birth. When I called him he was but one, and I blessed him and made him many. The LORD will surely comfort Zion and will look with compassion on all her ruins; He will make her deserts like Eden, her wastelands like the garden of the LORD. Joy and gladness will be found in her, thanksgiving and the sound of singing (Isaiah 51:1-3).

Hebron is the place where God's covenants with Abraham and his offspring become concrete. In Hebron, Abraham bought land. Also in Hebron the Lord demonstrated and manifested an intimate friendship with Abraham by visiting the tent of Abraham and Sarah to proclaim the birth of Isaac:

58

The LORD appeared to Abraham near the great trees of Mamre while he was sitting at the entrance of his tent in the heat of the day. Abraham looked up and saw three men standing nearby. When he saw them, he hurried from the entrance of his tent to meet them and bowed to the ground (Genesis 18:1, 2).

In Hebron, Isaac and Ishmael again met in the natural to bury their father Abraham. Because of the promise of the Abrahamic covenant, his seed, the sons of Isaac and Ishmael, are beginning to meet again to be reconciled as a blessing in the earth. Isaiah says look to your father Abraham.

Hebron, a city of refuge in Judea, was given to Caleb as an inheritance because of his faithfulness and good report.

They came back to Moses and Aaron and the whole Israelite community at Kadesh in the Desert of Paran. There they reported to them and to the whole assembly and showed the fruit of the land.

Then Caleb silenced the people before Moses and said, "We should go up and take possession of the land, for we can certainly do it."

But the men who had gone up with him said, "We can't attack those people, they are stronger than we are." And they spread among the Israelites a bad report about the land they had explored.

And [Caleb] said to the entire Israelite assembly, "The land we passed through and explored is exceedingly good. If the LORD is pleased with us, he will lead us into the land, a

land flowing with milk and honey, and will give it to us. Only do not rebel against the LORD. And do not be afraid of the people of the land, because we will swallow them up. Their protection is gone, but the LORD is with us. Do not be afraid of them (Numbers 13:26, 30-32; 14:7-9).

Like Abraham, Isaac, Jacob, and Caleb, David too moved in an intimate friendship with God. Hebron is the city where David was anointed as king of Judea and, later, king of a united Israel. It is where he reigned as king for seven years before his thirty-three year reign in Jerusalem. The first part of David's reign was in Hebron because of the significance of that city as a place of fatherhood and friendship. Then God brought him up to Jerusalem. By building his third altar in Hebron and his fourth altar in Jerusalem, Abraham prepared the way for David to rule as king in both Hebron and Jerusalem.

Noel Mann is one of our Gateway Coordinators in Australia. The fellowship he oversees was called Hebron. Now it is called Zion (Jerusalem). In the transformation of its name we can also see the progression from the third altar to the fourth altar from Hebron to Jerusalem.

In the past decades, many hostilities have existed between Jews and Muslims in Hebron. During the Mufti-inspired riots of 1929 many of the small remnant of Jews living in Hebron were slaughtered. The survivors of the 1929 massacres straggled back, but a fresh outburst in 1936 drove the remaining Jews from Hebron. Until 1967, there were no Jews in Hebron, a place where Abraham built an altar and purchased land as a legal possession. It is also a shame to the Jewish people that in Hebron an orthodox Jew shot and killed Arab worshippers at the Tomb of the Patriarchs. Today there are weekly media reports of Jews and Arabs killing and dying in Hebron, including the November 2002 murder of twelve Israeli soldiers in an ambush in Hebron.

Gary Cooperberg is a Jewish leader who made *Aliyah* from the USA to Kiryat Arba/Hebron and is traveling through the States encouraging others Jews to come home, to make *Aliyah* to the places of the Fathers in Israel. He has friendship and support from Bible-believing American Christians who are helping him and have an office for him in their church in Florida. Recently, some Arabs in Hebron are beginning to trust only in the one true God, the God of Israel, and in His covenants.

Emil, an Egyptian pastor, was fighting in the Six-Day War in 1967 against Israel and had many friends killed. There in the desert a great light appeared to him and took him into a trance where he saw Jesus who said to him, "I will protect you and take you back to Egypt to tell my people Egypt and the whole world I love them." Years later during the Yom Kippur War he was filled with anger and a great hatred of Israel grew within him. He decided not to preach from the Old Testament any longer, but only from the New Testament. Then one day, he was going to preach on love and the Holy Spirit said, "How can you preach on love and hate Israel?"

Emil told me:

I told the Lord of the hatred in my life, how it had become such a huge part of me and how it was a terrible battle. I knelt down and began to pray, asking the Lord to heal me. I said, "But Lord, if you can heal me, I am here." Suddenly, a wave like cold water swept from the top of my head and washed down into my being. It flowed into my heart and took away my hatred. I felt such a great joy! I was healed!

A few months later, I received an invitation from Israel to share at a convocation. As I landed at the Tel Aviv airport I began to cry. I was not only stepping into the land I have always wanted to tread, but I was also coming face to face with the fears and ill-feelings I carried in my heart about Israel. I was met at the airport by an Israeli leader. He came toward me and we introduced ourselves. HE HUGGED ME AND I HUGGED HIM. Finally, the hatred was gone. I knew Jesus had reconciled me to the Jewish people. Praise the Lord who removed the wall between the Jews and the gentiles then and now!

I love Jerusalem. I don't know what attracts me so much, but I especially love the walls of Jerusalem. I love walking around the walls and through the gates of Jerusalem. I love to just spend time talking with the people there inside the gates. Whenever I go to Jerusalem, I go to the Dome of the Rock, kneel with my Arab brothers and rebuke the spirit of deception over the Arabs. Then I go to the Holy Sepulchre and rebuke the spirits of tradition and religiosity amongst Christians. Also, I go to David's tomb and pray for the Jews. I always go to these three places and pray to God for deliverance. I believe in the Holy Spirit and I believe in the freedom that comes only through the Holy Spirit.

Chapter 7

The Mount Moriah/ Jerusalem Covenantal Promise Altar

Jerusalem is first mentioned in Genesis 14, when Abraham meets Melchizedek, King of Salem and priest of the Most High God.

> **Then Melchizedek king of Salem brought out bread and wine. He was priest of God Most High, and he blessed Abram, saying, "Blessed be Abram by God Most High, Creator of heaven and earth. And blessed be God Most High, who delivered your enemies into your hand." Then Abram gave him a tenth of everything (Genesis 14:18-20).**

The second mention of Jerusalem is when God tells Abraham to take his son Isaac to Mt. Moriah, believed to be Jerusalem, and offer him as a sacrifice. The altar built on Mt. Moriah is the most significant altar, because the ram of sacrifice is a picture of the Passover Lamb.

> **Then God said, "Take your son, your only son, Isaac, whom you love, and go to the region of Moriah. Sacrifice him there as a burnt offering on one of the mountains I will tell you about."**
> **Early the next morning Abraham got up and saddled his donkey. He took with him two of his servants and his son Isaac. When he had cut enough wood for the burnt offering, he set out for**

the place God had told him about. On the third day Abraham looked up and saw the place in the distance. He said to his servants, "Stay here with the donkey while I and the boy go over there. We will worship, and then we will come back to you" (Genesis 22:2-5).

Abraham was giving the life of his promised son that he had waited for until he was almost a hundred years old. That was a miracle. He was offering up his son as worship, unto God. He thought he was going to kill his son. He said, "...we are going to worship God." If God were to ask you to sacrifice your life and your son as worship, would you do so? Abraham was willing. Abraham was so committed to God's covenant that he realized even if he killed his son in worship, his son would be raised from the dead to fulfill God's covenantal promise forever. Isaac, his son, was born out of a miracle and if God performs one miracle he can perform another one. It is true love-worship to be willing to lay down the lives of our sons and our own lives as worship unto the Lord. The story continues:

Abraham answered, "God himself will provide the lamb for the burnt offering, my son." And the two of them went together.

When they reached the place God had told him about, Abraham built an altar there and arranged the wood on it. He bound his son Isaac and laid him on the altar, on top of the wood. Then he reached out his hand and took the knife to slay his son. But the angel of the LORD called out to him from heaven, "Abraham! Abraham!"

"Here I am," he replied.

"Do not lay a hand on the boy," he said. "Do not do anything to him. Now I know that you

64

fear God, because you have not withheld from me your son, your only son."

Abraham looked up and there in a thicket he saw a ram caught by its horns. He went over and took the ram and sacrificed it as a burnt offering instead of his son. So Abraham called that place The LORD Will Provide. And to this day it is said, "On the mountain of the LORD it will be provided" (Genesis 22:8-14).

David's Covenant Altar in Jerusalem

Abraham was not the only one who built an altar on the mountains of Moriah. King David did as well. David not only built an altar, but also purchased land from Araunah the Jebusite where the temple and its altar were built thereafter.

When the angel stretched out his hand to destroy Jerusalem, the LORD was grieved because of the calamity and the LORD said to the angel who was afflicting the people, "Enough! Withdraw your hand." The angel of the LORD was then at the threshing-floor of Araunah the Jebusite.

When David saw the angel who was striking down the people, he said to the LORD, "I am the one who has sinned and done wrong. These are but sheep. What have they done? Let your hand fall upon me and my family."

On that day Gad went to David and said to him, "Go up and build an altar to the LORD on the threshing-floor of Araunah the Jebusite." So David went up, as the LORD had commanded through Gad. When Araunah looked and saw the

king and his men coming towards him, he went out and bowed down before the king with his face to the ground.

Araunah said, "Why has my lord the king come to his servant?"

"To buy your threshing-floor," David answered, "so that I can build an altar to the LORD, that the plague on the people may be stopped."

Araunah said to David, "Let my lord the king take whatever pleases him and offer it up. Here are oxen for the burnt offering, and here are the threshing-sledges and the ox yokes for the wood. O king, Araunah gives all this to the king." Araunah also said to him, "May the LORD your God accept you" (2 Samuel 24:16-23).

Opposing Araunah's request, David did not accept the land, the wood, the animals, or the grain as a free gift, but bore their price by buying it for fifty shekels of silver.

But the king replied to Araunah, "No, I insist on paying you for it, I will not sacrifice to the LORD my God burnt offerings that cost me nothing."

So David bought the threshing-floor and the oxen and paid fifty shekels of silver for them. David built an altar to the LORD there and sacrificed burnt offerings and fellowship offerings. Then the LORD answered prayer on behalf of the land, and the plague on Israel was stopped (2 Samuel 24:24, 25).

Then David said, "The house of the LORD God is to be here, and also the altar of burnt offerings for Israel" (1 Chronicles 22:1).

Then Solomon began to build the temple of the LORD in Jerusalem on Mount Moriah, where the LORD had appeared to his father David. It was on the threshing-floor of Araunah [Ornan] the Jebusite, the place provided by David (2 Chronicles 3:1).

An Arab leader, Afeef, from Moab, Jordan, a Moabite like Ruth, rejects replacement theology and now embraces the God of Israel and His covenants with the land and people of Israel. He is even training other Arab believers to do the same! In 2002, at the *All Nations Convocation Jerusalem*, an Arab leader in Jerusalem gave a model of the Old City to a believing Jewish leader saying, "I give this to you as a prophetic act that Jerusalem belongs to you." In June 1967, Israel and Jerusalem were attacked by the surrounding Arab nations in the Six-Day War. As a result, the Jews again regained the Old City.

Jews believe Messiah, the Son of David, will take up the throne of David as Isaiah 9:7 says and Christians believe that Messiah was the ultimate sacrifice offered on the Temple Mount, Mt. Moriah, in Jerusalem. We know that very soon, as we read in Ezekiel 48, the Lord will be there, or, we could say the Lord will be here, in Jerusalem, on the Temple Mount. He will reign from this place. Ezekiel 43 says that it will be the place of the soles of His feet forever, and all things in heaven and earth are united as one in Messiah.

Son of Man, this is the place of my throne and the place of the soles of my feet [the temple]. This is where I will live among the Israelites for ever. I will live among them for ever (Ezekiel 43:7).

67

Shechem, Beth El, Hebron and Jerusalem are four places where God made covenants with Israel in regard to the land of Israel and in regard to the salvation of Israel through the Messiah, through the Jewish people, through the son of David. He also made covenants with Israel that Abraham's seed will be as plentiful as the dust of the earth and the stars of heaven.

Abraham saw the salvation of the nations coming when he envisioned the nations grafted into the commonwealth of Israel. The nations are grafted into Abraham. The nations are grafted into the land of Israel. The nations are grafted into the covenants of God with Abraham. Praise God we are seeing the fullness of the gentiles come in, and the fullness of Israel will be grafted into one olive tree.

The natural children of Abraham are the Jews and the Arabs. We are about to see the natural seed of Abraham also become the spiritual offspring of Abraham. God wants to graft the Jewish people into the New Covenant because they are the natural seed (Jer 31:31-34). We live in the days of restoration. As you are praying through the twelve gateways for the fullness of the gentiles in your gateway, pray also for Israel and the fullness of Isaiah 19 that Egypt, Israel and Assyria will worship God together as a blessing in the midst of the earth.

Jewish-Arab Reconciliation in Jerusalem

We are so grateful to see four-hundred and fifty Jewish and Arab youth worshiping the Covenant God of Israel here in Israel as a prophetic sign of what God is going to do in the midst of this whole situation. It is a testimony to God's covenant-keeping faithfulness that at this time, in all these terrible challenges, they would be able to come together to worship. This is only the first fruit towards what God is going to do. I believe for the fullness.

On the edge of the Mount of Olives is Ma'ale Adumim, a city of 60,000 Jews, the largest city in Judea and Samaria and a part of greater Jerusalem. The Mayor of Ma'ale Adumim, Benny Kashriel, is a friend of mine and, as an act of reconciliation between Jews and gentiles, wants to build a Good Samaritan Inn in the area where the story took place near Ma'ale Adumim. You may want to help by praying for and investing in this Inn being built for many tourists worldwide, that it will help to build bridges of reconciliation in Israel. The following is the story of the Good Samaritan from Luke 10:25-37:

On one occasion an expert in the law stood up to test Jesus. "Teacher," he asked, "what must I do to inherit eternal life?"

"What is written in the Law?" he replied. "How do you read it?"

He answered: " 'Love the Lord your God with all your heart and with all your soul and with all your strength and with all your mind'; and, 'Love your neighbor as yourself.' "

"You have answered correctly," Jesus replied. "Do this and you will live."

But he wanted to justify himself, so he asked Jesus, "And who is my neighbor?"

In reply Jesus said: "A man was going down from Jerusalem to Jericho, when he fell into the hands of robbers. They stripped him of his clothes, beat him and went away, leaving him half-dead. A priest happened to be going down the same road, and when he saw the man, he passed by on the other side. So too, a Levite, when he came to the place and saw him, passed by on the other side. But a Samaritan [like an Arab today], as he traveled, came where the man was; and when he saw him, he took pity on him. He went to him and bandaged his wounds, pouring

on oil and wine. Then he put the man on his own donkey, brought him to an inn and took care of him. The next day he took out two silver coins and gave them to the innkeeper. 'Look after him,' he said, 'and when I return, I will reimburse you for any extra expense you may have.'

"Which of these three do you think was a neighbor to the man who fell into the hands of the robbers?"

The expert in the law replied, "The one who had mercy on him."

Jesus told him, "Go and do likewise."

We are now seeing the seeds of foundational altars so that they can be fully resurrected and restored in Shechem, Beth El, Hebron and Jerusalem. We need to pray for blindness to be removed from the eyes of the first son of Abraham, the curse to be broken, and that the Jews will embrace God's covenant and enter into the fullness of God's blessings through Abraham, which God proclaimed they will enter into. The God of Israel is a covenant-keeping God forever.

The altars are going to be rebuilt in the heartland of Israel—the heartland of Judea and Samaria. Pray that God will restore the national and heart foundations of Israel in Shechem, Beth El, Hebron, and Jerusalem. The covenants are not only with the Jews or only with the Arabs in the natural and spiritual, but they are also with the nations of the earth in Messiah because these covenants were released to and through father Abraham when he built the altars. If there is any hope for *shalom/salaam* in Jerusalem before Messiah's coming, it will only happen as Jews and Arabs in these places recognize and receive revelation of the God of Israel and His covenants, and worship Him together (Isaiah 19:23-25).

Jerusalem, The United Capital of Israel

Under King David, King Solomon, and for most of the next thousand years, Jerusalem was the united capital of Israel until the time of Jesus. Throughout history Jerusalem has never been the capital of the Arab or the Palestinian people, only the Jewish people from 996 BCE to 587 BCE, from 513 BCE to 70 CE, and again from 1967 to the present. For one thousand thirty-two years Jerusalem has been the capital of Israel.

The majority of people in Jerusalem in the last two hundred years have been Jewish, not Muslim. According to the first official public census in 1844 there were 7,120 Jews and 5,768 Arabs living in the city of Jerusalem. By 1990 there were 353,000 Jews and 124,000 Arabs. In the year 2003, there were 688,900 people living in Jerusalem, of whom about 30% (206,670 people) are Arabs (Statistics from *Israel's Bureau of Statistics*, 2004).

During the Six Day War in 1967, while Israeli soldiers repelled attacks by surrounding Arab nations, they entered Jerusalem from the Mount of Olives through the Lion's Gate, thus taking Jerusalem. Jerusalem was again reunited as the capital of Israel. Jesus prophesied this would happen in Luke 21:24, **"Jerusalem will be trampled upon by the Gentiles until the times of the Gentiles are fulfilled."** Matthew 5:35 says Jerusalem is the city of the Great King.

In Zechariah 12:3 it says all nations will come against Jerusalem, but Jerusalem will be an immovable rock for all nations and all who try to move it will injure themselves. God will destroy all nations who attack Jerusalem. Zechariah 14:12 says a plague will strike all who fought against Jerusalem—the flesh, the eyes, and tongues will rot. God says He will watch over Judah-Jerusalem, but blind the nations who attack her.

The everlasting covenant that the God of Israel made with Abraham is with the whole land of Canaan, but the place of His throne where He will reign from and the place of the soles of His feet forever is Mt. Moriah. This is where Abraham offered Isaac in

71

Genesis 22, and where David bought the threshing floor for fifty shekels of silver three thousand years ago (II Samuel 24:24-25). It is also where Solomon's temple stood and where Christians believe Jesus was lifted up making a new covenant (Jeremiah 31:31-37) that for them brings fulfilment of God's covenant with Abraham in Genesis 12:3 and Genesis 15 that all nations will be blessed through his seed.

This everlasting covenant that God made with Abraham is central for the throne of the King of Jerusalem forever, for the natural and spiritual redemption of Israel, and the reunification and restoration of Jerusalem. This will ultimately be the place of the soles of His feet among the Israelites (Ezekiel 43:1-7).

PART III

The Abrahamic Covenant for Believing Israel and Believers in all Nations

The Olive Tree-
The House of Abraham and
The House of David

Chapter 8

Children of Abraham by Faith

God's Abrahamic Covenant-promises not only focus on and emphasize the land of Israel, but also relate to God's original and ongoing purpose of redeeming and saving Israel and the Church in the nations. Through the Abrahamic Covenant, the people of God (Jews) cannot only inherit the land, but salvation also. The God of Israel made a covenant with Abraham in Genesis 16:18 and later said, "My covenant I establish with Isaac" in Genesis 17:21. He also established covenant with Jacob-Israel in Genesis 28:13-14, and in Genaesis 35:10 with Israel and a community of nations who are those who beleive, the children (sons) of Abraham by faith. God's redemptive purpose (covenants) for the nations (gentiles) was born out of the God of Israel's covenant with His first-born son, Israel.

Believers from the nations are one with believing Jews in the inheritance of salvation, and oneness of purpose and destiny joined together in the Olive Tree preparing for Messiah's coming and the coming of the New Jerusalem down from Heaven that Abraham was looking for (Hebrews 11:10).

The Abrahamic Covenant-promise for the land of Israel and the children of Abraham by faith was given to Abraham beginning in Genesis 12:1-3 (Emphasis added):

> **The LORD had said to Abram, "Leave your country, your people and your father's household and go to the land I will show you. I will make you into a great nation and I will bless you; I will make your name great, and you will be a blessing. I will**

bless those who bless you, and whoever curses you I will curse; and ALL PEOPLES [nations] ON EARTH WILL BE BLESSED THROUGH YOU.

Abraham returns to Beth El where previously he had built an altar (Genesis 12:6):

The LORD said to Abram after Lot had parted from him, "Lift up your eyes from where you are and look north and south, east and west. All the land that you see I will give to you and your offspring forever. I WILL MAKE YOUR OFFSPRING [lit. seed] LIKE THE DUST OF THE EARTH, SO THAT IF ANYONE COULD COUNT THE DUST, THEN YOUR OFFSPRING [lit. seed] COULD BE COUNTED (Genesis 13:14-16, Emphasis added).

All Nations on Earth Blessed through Yeshua and Father Abraham

God's Abrahamic Covenant-promises not only focus on and emphasize the land of Israel, but also relate to God's original and ongoing purpose of redeeming and saving Israel and the Church in the nations. Through the Abrahamic Covenant, the people of God (Jews) cannot only inherit the land, but salvation also. The God of Israel made a covenant with Abraham in Genesis 16:18 and later said, "My covenant I establish with Isaac" in Genesis 17:21. He also established covenant with Jacob-Israel in Genesis 28:13-14, and in Genaesis 35:10 with Israel and a community of nations who are those who beleive, the children (sons) of Abraham by faith. God's redemptive purpose (covenants) for the nations (gentiles) was born out of the God of Israel's covenant with His first-born son, Israel.

76

In Genesis 11 man is described as trying to build a tower of Babel (lit. gate of a god) to Heaven, but failed because it was man's initiative and the heavens were closed. God then confused them and scattered them. In Genesis 14:13, when Abraham passed over the Euphrates into the Promised Land, he was called a "Hebrew," which means "to cross or pass over or between." He "crossed over" the Euphrates from Babel (Babylon) to Beth El (called the gate of Heaven) and made a covenant with God-Yeshua in the person of Melchizedek.

It appears it was his obedience and willingness to cross over from Babel to Bethel that made him a "Hebrew," to be declared righteous by faith, and to inherit the Promised Land. By crossing over he entered the Promised Land and entered into a covenant with the Root-Yeshua, the Hebrew of Hebrews, King of Righteousness, King of Peace (Salem-Jerusalem), and King of the Jews.

In Beth El, contrary to Babel, God took the initiative with Abraham and later with Jacob to rend the heavens and come down. Abraham the "Hebrew" later "passed through" the whole land of promise from Assyria to Israel to Egypt and back to Israel. Later those who believed in Yeshua-God of Israel, led by Joshua, crossed over again from Egypt back to the covenanted Promised Land to take possession of it.

When God made a covenant with Abraham (Genesis 15), He said that a smoking firepot and blazing torch 'passed between' the pieces. In Isaiah 62:1 it says Jerusalem's salvation will be like a blazing torch. Truly the New Covenant is the key to opening up the way to salvation as Yeshua 'passed over' from heaven to earth and from death to life (John 5:24) to bring salvation.

In Jerusalem, after Abraham crossed over from what today is Iraq, he had an encounter with the King of Jerusalem, Melchizedek-Yeshua who is the God of Israel revealed as the King of Righteousness and Peace, which radically changed his life. This is emphasized by the fact that the Gospel was preached to him in advance (Galatians 3:8) and that he was declared righteous (Genesis 15:6).

77

Melchizedek-Yeshua   (lit. King of Righteousness) broke bread and wine with Abraham and blessed him as He did again two thousand years later in Jerusalem with His disciples just before His ascension. After Melchizedek-Yeshua breaks bread and wine and blesses Abraham, Abraham does three things: He tithes to Him, raises his hand, and makes an oath (covenant) with the King of Righteousness. Melchizedek-Yeshua then declared Abraham righteous because of his faith and obvious belief in God's covenant and the Lord Yeshua, who is the only one who can justify us and makes us righteous. Righteousness was imputed to Abraham, his physical descendants (Jews), and spiritual descendants (Christians) who trust in Messiah (Genesis 14, 15; Romans 11). Even today, in these days of fullness and restoration, these spiritual descendants are proclaimed righteous and grafted into the cultivated olive tree whose root is Yeshua.

Understand, then, that those who believe [Jews and Gentiles who have faith] are children of Abraham (Galatians 3:7).

Melchizedek-Yeshua's covenant with Abraham is the biblical foundation of His and our Jewish-Hebraic roots. Hebrews 7:9-10 says even Levi, the High Priest during the time of Joshua, who under the Law collected tithes, paid a tenth through Abraham to Melchizedek. In Psalm 110:1 the Holy Spirit through David says, "The LORD said to my Lord [Yeshua]: 'Sit at my right hand until I make your enemies a footstool for your feet.'" David emphasizes this further by saying, "The LORD has sworn and will not change his mind, 'You [Messiah Yeshua] are a priest [and king] forever in the order of Melchizedek'" (v. 4).

The New Covenant is the fulfilment of the Abrahamic Covenant, the covenant Melchizedek-Yeshua made with Abraham (Genesis 14 & 15) that will culminate in fullness when Yeshua begins His reign forever on David's Throne on the Temple Mount. Yeshua is the guarantee of a better covenant, the covenant (oath) Yeshua authored with our father Abraham. Yeshua's death brings fullness to the better covenant, as the Lamb of God is the fulfilment of the ram replacing Isaac on the mountains of Moriah/Jerusalem. The author of Hebrews says Yeshua is the author and fulfilment of our faith (v.12:2). It is being brought from first-fruits into fullness (fulfilment) as the Messiah through the Holy Spirit is now revealed as Christ in us the Hope of Glory (Jeremiah 31:31-34; Hebrews 8:8-13).

It seems as if Abraham saw the death, crucifixion, and resurrection of Yeshua as Yeshua says in John 8:56, 58, "Your father Abraham rejoiced at the thought of seeing my day; and saw it and was glad." In the song, *Behold the Lamb*, it says Yeshua was slain before the foundation of the world. As I understand, at the crucifixion/resurrection they sang: This is the day that the Lord has made we will and be glad and rejoice in it. Hebrews 11:10 says Abraham was also looking forward to the city with foundations, whose architect and builder is God so apparently he not only had a vision of the crucifixion and resurrection, but also the New Jerusalem coming down from heaven.

The New Covenant is the fulfilment of the Abrahamic Covenant, the covenant Melchizedek-Yeshua made with Abraham

Abraham, who came out of the region of Babel encountered Yeshua as the King of Jerusalem. He realized that Melchizedek-Yeshua was everything, would provide everything, and refused to take anything from the King of Sodom, but interceded for a few righteous ones to be delivered to the eternal Covenant God of righteousness, the King of Jerusalem.

Abraham did not waver in certainty regarding the promise of God, but was strengthened in his faith and gave glory to God being fully persuaded that God had the power to do what He promised! He wants to do the same for us as He credits us with righteousness, as we believe in the Covenant God of Israel who raised Jesus from the dead! Abraham was declared righteous because of his faith. Paul in Galatians 3:6 says, "Consider Abraham: 'He believed God,

79

and it was credited to Him as righteousness' [also Genesis 15:6; & Romans 4:3, 22]."

Circumcision was a sign or seal of righteousness, but did not create it. Righteousness came by faith while Abraham was still uncircumcised. Abraham is the father of all who believe, both circumcised and uncircumcised. All who walk in the fellowship of the faith that our father Abraham had, even before he was circumcised, are children of Abraham by faith. The promise came by faith and is guaranteed to all of Abraham's offspring. Abraham is the father of all of us who believe. We are not called the children of Moses by faith, or the children of Israel by faith, or the children of David by faith, or even the children of Jesus by faith. All believers are called the children of Abraham by faith, because the spiritual seed of covenantal promise, for salvation of Jews and gentiles from the nations came from Yeshua through Abraham. When Yeshua spoke to the Pharisees and Sadducees he understood that being a descendant of Abraham was not a means to righteousness in itself, but pointed to the inheritance of Abraham's faith,

> **Do not begin to say to yourselves, "We have Abraham for our father." For I tell you that out of these stones God can raise up children for Abraham (Luke 3:8).**

Abraham—Father of Many Nations and Father of the House of Prayer for All Nations

God's revelation and original intention through Abraham was to have Israel and a community of nations. It appears that (Yeshua) Melchizedek birthed the seed of the house of prayer for all nations through Abraham, the great intercessor, almost four thousand years ago as it is written about Abraham, "I have made you the father of MANY NATIONS" (Genesis 17:4, 5, Emphasis added). God

Almighty said to Jacob-Israel, "A nation and a COMMUNITY OF NATIONS [HOPFAN] will come from you" (Genesis 35:11, emphasis added). Later, Solomon's Temple was called a house of prayer for ALL NATIONS (Isaiah 56:7). Then Yeshua says in Mark 11:17 more than one thousand years later, "My House will be called a house of prayer for ALL NATIONS." Now in the twentieth and twenty-first century, He is again building his house of prayer for All Nations in Jerusalem, Israel and in all nations of the world.

The house of prayer for all nations was conceived by Yeshua, the Root of the Olive Tree, through Abraham, a great intercessor and father of many nations. The house of prayer for all nations was conceived with Abraham because the God of Israel first made covenant with him. He is our father in the sight of God in whom we believe. Against all hope, Abraham's hope believed and he became the father of many nations!

All that believe, both Jews and gentiles, are children of Abraham by faith. The scriptures promise that God would justify the gentiles by faith, and announced the Gospel in advance to Abraham, "All nations [the gentiles] will be blessed through you" (Genesis 12: 3). Therefore those who have faith are blessed along with Abraham, the man of faith.

He redeemed us in order that the blessing given to Abraham might come to the Gentiles through Christ Jesus, so that by faith we might receive the promise of the Spirit (Galatians 3:14).

God in His grace gave the promise of the seed to Abraham for all nations.

Through your offspring [lit. Seed] ALL NATIONS on earth will be blessed, because you have obeyed my voice (Genesis 22:18, Emphasis added).

81

If you belong to Christ, then you are Abraham's seed, and heirs according to the promise (Galatians 3:29).

In Genesis 17:16 God says to Abraham, "I will bless her [Sarah] and I will surely give you a son by her. I will bless her so that she will be the mother of nations; kings of peoples will come from her." Isaac was supernaturally and miraculously born by the Holy Spirit when Abraham was one hundred years old. Genesis 17:19 says:

Your wife Sarah will bear you a son, and you will call him Isaac. I will establish my covenant with him as an everlasting covenant for his descendants after him.

The seed of Messiah was carried to and through Abraham, Isaac, and Jacob onward, thus preparing the way for the birth of Yeshua.

The promises were spoken to Abraham and to his seed [also Genesis 12:7; 13:15, 16; 22:18; 24:7]. The Scripture does not say, "and to seeds," meaning many people, but "and to your seed," meaning one person who is Christ (Galatians 3:16).

All Nations on Earth Blessed through Yeshua and Jacob-Israel

Jacob-Israel also had an encounter with the God of Israel/Yeshua. Babel represents Babylon and man's futile initiative trying to reach heaven paving the way to hell. Beth El, called the Gate of Heaven, represents God's Gate to and from Heaven and God's initiative to rend Heaven and come down to Jacob-Israel on earth in Beth El.

In Beth El Jacob saw the stairway of heaven on earth and saw standing above it the God of Israel, the Lord Yeshua.

> **Jacob left Beersheba and set out for Haran. When he reached a certain place, he stopped for the night because the sun had set. Taking one of the stones there, he put it under his head and lay down to sleep. He had a dream in which he saw a stairway resting on the earth, with its top reaching to heaven, and the angels of God were ascending and descending on it. There above it stood the LORD, and he said: "I am the LORD, the God of your father Abraham and the God of Isaac. I will give you and your descendants the land on which you are lying. Your descendants will be like the dust of the earth, and you will spread out to the west and to the east, to the north and to the south. ALL THE PEOPLES ON THE EARTH WILL BE BLESSED THROUGH YOU AND YOUR OFFSPRING [lit. Seed]. I am with you and will watch over you wherever you go, and I will bring you back to this land. I will not leave you until I have done what I have promised you."**
>
> **When Jacob awoke from his sleep, he thought, "Surely the LORD is in this place, and I was not aware of it." He was afraid and said, "How awesome is this place! This is none other than the house of God [Beth El]; this is the gate of heaven"** (Genesis 28:10-17, Emphasis added).

It is a thirty minute drive from Beth El to Jerusalem where on the Mount of Olives, Yeshua ascended to heaven and will descend at his Second Coming as the angels ascended and descended in Beth El. In John 1:51 Yeshua prophetically speaks of this when He says,

"I tell you the truth, you shall see heaven open, and the angels of God ascending and descending on the Son of Man."

Beth El - Gate to Heaven
The House of God is
the House of Prayer for All Nations

When Jacob sees an open heaven in Beth El, God then changes his name to Israel.

> **God said to him, "Your name is Jacob, but you will no longer be called Jacob; your name will be Israel." So he named him Israel. And God said to him, "I am God Almighty, be fruitful and increase in number. A NATION AND A COMMUNITY OF NATIONS WILL COME FROM YOU, and kings will come from your body" (Genesis 35:10, 11, Emphasis added).**

I believe Jacob did not buy land at Beth El because here he had a revelation of Yeshua, the God of Israel, in heaven, but he also saw his covenant with Yeshua from heaven, and probably saw his ultimate citizenship in heaven in the New Jerusalem. The heartland (Genesis 13:14-16), whole land (Genesis 15:18), and whole earth were promised to him from heaven. The vision was of all nations on earth being blessed through him and his offspring through the house of prayer, not only for Israel, but for all nations as well. At Babel man tried to build a tower to heaven, but failed. When God made covenant with Abraham and met Jacob at Beth El, He rent the heavens, opened the gate of heaven, and brought heaven down to him.

The house of prayer for all nations was conceived in the covenat Yeshua, the Root of the Olive Tree, made with Abraham, the father of many nations.

Our roots as Christians do not begin with Golgotha, or the Garden Tomb, the Upper Room, or the Apostles. Our Jewish-Hebraic roots begins with the God of Israel-Yeshua's promise and covenant to us through Abraham and later in Jacob-Israel in Beth El, the House of God. This is the place of the roots of our faith in Yeshua through Abraham, the man of faith and father of us all, and Jacob, whose name was earlier changed to Israel. Through Abraham's, Isaac's, and Jacob's offspring (seed), Israel and the Church in the nations were born and blessed. The seed for the Church, the house of prayer for ALL NATIONS, was born out of Israel in Beth El.

THE OLIVE TREE

YESHUA is the Author and Finisher (Fulfillment or Fullness) of our faith (Hebrews 6:11)

YESHUA says:"I am the Alpha and Omega." (Rev. 1:8)

YESHUA is the First and the Last, the Beginning and the End (Rev. 22: 13)

YESHUA says:"I am the Root and Offspring of David, the bright and Morning Star" (Rev. 22:16; Isa. 9:7). He will reign on the throne of David.

Natural branches never cut off!

Fullness of the Natural Jewish Branches grafted back in! (Rom. 11:12)

Fullness of the Wild Gentile Branches grafted in! (Rom. 11:25-26)

YESHUA is both the Author of our faith in the Abrahamic Covenant and the fulfillment in His death, burial and rueeurec-tion in the New Covenant.

The first-fruits is seen in the Kingdoms of David and Solomon and the fullness will be in YESHUA's riegn on David's Throne on the Temple Mount forever.

YESHUA- Reigning on the Throne of David forever

YESHUA- New Covenant

DAVID

ISRAEL

JACOB

ISAAC

SEED OF ABRAHAM

YESHUA'S COVENANT WITH ABRAHAM

YESHUA IS THE ROOT OF THE OLIVE TREE & FIRST FRUITS

Melchizedek-YESHUA, The King of Righteousness imputed righteousness to Abraham because of Abraham's faith (Gen. 14,15).

Yeshua said:"Before Abraham was, I AM" and "Abraham saw my day and was glad." (John 6)

Chapter 9

Last Days Restoration and Blessing of the Sons of Abraham in the Olive Tree—House of God

God laid the foundations of His ultimate redemptive purpose through Abraham almost four thousand years ago, because he found a man of faith who Melchizedek-Yeshua could be revealed to who would begin preparing the foundation and way for the last day restoration. This is why in Isaiah 51:1-3 it does not say we should look to Adam or Noah or Isaac or Jacob or Moses or David or John the Baptist as our father, but it says we should look to Abraham our father. Abraham's heart was to see his sons, both of whom he loved, reconciled as one in the God of Israel. Although his sons met together to bury him in Hebron, Abraham had to wait for Yeshua's death and resurrection to make the "One New Man" of Jews and Arab-gentiles and wait for the heavenly Father's time in these last days for this to begin to happen. As high and holy of a purpose that this is, it also has brought satanic-Islamic counter-attacks of terrorism against God's holy purpose. But the purpose of God shall ultimately prevail. However, the restoration of the natural sons of Abraham could not fully have begun until Israel was born in 1948, because the natural restoration of Israel had to proceed the spiritual restoration of Egypt, Israel, and Assyria. In other words, the Isaiah 19 Highway through Egypt, Israel and Assyria could not be built before Israel was restored.

In these last days of restoration, we see God doing two things. First, He is bringing to faith the fullness of the gentiles from all nations that He calls the children of Abraham by faith. Today, there are one to two billion gentile-Christian children of Abraham by faith in the world.

The second thing God is doing is bringing the natural sons and daughters of Abraham, the Jews and the Arabs, to the faith of Abraham also through Abraham's Seed, Yeshua, and reconciling them as One New Man in Yeshua, the Prince of Peace. We have already seen the first-fruits of Egypt, Israel and Assyria, Arabs and Jews, worshiping God together as a blessing in the midst of the earth (Isaiah 19:23-25). Recently the Lord said we need to pray for the natural children of Abraham to become the spiritual sons of Abraham like the stars of the sky. We will see fullness come. The more this happens, the more a great blessing will be released to all nations in the midst of the earth. This will prepare the way for the greatest harvest in history and prepare the way for Messiah's coming.

We see in Romans 11:1 Paul says, "I am an Israelite, a descendant of Abraham." He goes on to say in verses 11 and 12:

Because of their [the Jews] transgression, salvation has come to the Gentiles to make Israel envious. But if their transgression means riches for the world and their loss means riches for the Gentiles, how much greater riches will their [the Jews'] fullness bring!

Paul goes on to talk about a cultivated olive tree saying some of its natural branches (Jews) have been broken off because of unbelief. Today, in our day of restoration, God is grafting these branches back into this olive tree. Paul also says that the gentiles are wild olive shoots taken out of another olive tree that is wild by nature. In the natural, Ishmael represents the gentiles (a wild olive tree and its shoots and branches) as a wild donkey of a man (Genesis 16:11-12). However Ishmael (representing Egypt, Assyria and the Arabs) was circumcised with Abraham, which is a sign that he is destined to belong in the house of Abraham. I believe that the redemptive purpose of the Arabs is to lead a paradigm shift of the nations (gentile branches) out of the wild olive tree to be grafted into the cultivated Olive Tree, the house of Abraham that they were once thrown out of. The destiny of the Arabs is to lead the gentiles as Ruth, a Moabite (representing Arab nations today), did saying to the people of Isreal, "Your people shall be my people, and your God, my God; where you will go I will go and where you will lie I will lie (Ruth 1:16)." The believing branches from the wild olive tree are being taken out and grafted into the cultivated olive tree and now have the nurturing sap of the cultivated olive root, which is Abraham's and our Root, Yeshua.

There is much false and confused teaching on "Jewish Roots" today that is leading many astray to believe that the Law can justify that our roots are in Judaism, leading some even to deny Yeshua. Any teaching on "Jewish Roots" recognizing works or anything other than faith in Yeshua, the King of Righteousness, Peace and the Jews, as the ultimate Root and foundation of the faith is a false foundation. In Galatians 3:11 Paul says, "Clearly no one is justified before God by the Law, 'Because the righteous will live by faith.'" If our Jewish roots are in works or anything other than faith in Yeshua, the King of Righteousness, and the grace of God, then it is a bitter root like Esau partook of, which leads to destruction (Hebrews 12:14-16). Deuteronomy 19:19 says in Hebrew that one must purge the root of evil from among your house.

I believe the redemptive purpose of Arabs is to lead a paradigm shift of the nations—gentile branches—out of the wild olive tree and grafted into the cultivated Olive Tree.

We must realize that Yeshua is the Root of Abraham and that we do not support the root by our self-righteousness, pharisaical holiness and goodness, but Yeshua, The Root and Holy One of Israel, supports us by His redemptive grace and by us partaking of His holiness and righteousness by faith. The only way a Jew or gentile can become and remain a part of the cultivated olive tree is by faith in Yeshua the Messiah, the Root of Abraham, Jacob-Israel, David, and all believers.

> **So then, just as you received Christ Jesus as Lord, continue to live in him, rooted and built up in him, strengthened in the faith as you were taught, and overflowing with thankfulness (Colossians 2:6, 7).**

Romans 11:16 says, "If the first-fruits...and if the root [Yeshua] is holy, so are the branches." Yeshua Melchizedek imputed righteousness and holiness to us through the Abrahamic covenant as the root of the olive tree to make all branches, both Jewish and gentiles, righteous and holy.

Paul continues:

> **Israel has experienced a hardening in part until the fullness of the Gentiles has come in [to the olive tree] (Romans 11:25) [joining the fullness of the Jews-Israel into their own olive tree (Romans 11:12, 23, 24)]. And so all Israel will be saved (Romans 11:26).**

> **Peace and mercy to all who follow this rule, even to the Israel of God (Galatians 6:16).**

The fullness of Jewish and gentile branches will be grafted into the cultivated olive tree whose root is Messiah Yeshua and whose trunk is Abraham, Isaac, and Jacob-Israel. Yeshua said, "Before Abraham was born, I am."

The promise and covenant to Abraham and his seed from Yeshua (Melchizedek) is for the Jews, who are the chosen seed of Abraham naturally, who receive Messiah. The promise and covenant to Abraham and his seed from Yeshua (Melchizedek) is also for the Arabs who are natural children of Abraham and, by faith, becoming the children of Abraham spiritually. It also includes all gentiles (Christians) in the world who become children of Abraham by faith. We will all be part of the New Jerusalem forever, which father Abraham was looking forward to almost four thousand years ago. Because of the oath of the New Covenant sealed in the blood of Yeshua as a priest after the order of Melchizedek FOREVER! We will all be the sons of Abraham by faith in Yeshua The Root—The Alpha and Omega, The First and Last, The Beginning and the End, The Author and Finisher of our faith, The Root and Offspring of Abraham and David, The Bright Morning Star—forever.

He redeemed us in order that the blessing given to Abraham might [not only come to the Jews, but also] come to the Gentiles through Christ Jesus, so that by faith we might receive the [covenantal] promise of the Spirit (Galatians 3:14).

The House of David
The House, Heart, Tabernacle and Throne of David are Being Restored in the Olive Tree

The restoration of the House, Heart, Tabernacle, and Throne of David is the last stage of fulfilment in the Seed of God's covenant with Abraham preparing the way for the fullness of the cultivated olive tree and Messiah's coming. In Zechariah 12, the 'House of David' is mentioned five times in eight verses. Zechariah tells us that the most feeble believer in Jerusalem will be like David and the house of David like God (Zechariah 12:8). In Amos 9, God says that in the last days He will restore David's fallen tent (also called the Tabernacle of David). This is the nation of Israel, which is David's throne and Messiah's throne. God is also restoring the Tabernacle of David as 24-hour worship is established in Israel and worldwide.

God is going to do an awesome thing in changing the people of Jerusalem and Israel forever by changing their heart and spirit from Saul to the heart and spirit of David, which is the heart of God preparing for Messiah's coming. This will happen as they turn from the spirit of the Law, sin and death to the spirit of life and faith in Yeshua, The Root, and the law of the spirit of grace and truth. This is the only way we can be declared righteous, our hearts be circumcised, and have the heart of David.

At the triumphant entry of Yeshua on Palm Sunday, His disciples proclaimed, "Hosanna to the Son of David!" To worship the Lord, David, the seed of Abraham, Isaac and Jacob-Israel, purchased a threshing floor that later became the foundation for the Temple Mount. The Temple Mount is referred to as the Throne of David and the Throne of the Lord. It is the center of the Heartland of Israel—Judea and Samaria (Genesis 13:14-17), land that God promised forever to the descendants of Abraham, Isaac, and Jacob-Israel—and the whole land God covenanted to Abraham, David and Abraham's descendants forever in Genesis 15:18-20.

Isaiah 9:7 says that Messiah will sit on David's throne forever. The area of the Temple Mount is also the place where Yeshua, the Seed of Abraham and David died to bring fullness of righteousness to the Jews and Gentiles alike. The throne of David on the Temple Mount, where David had the vision to build the Temple, is also where Yeshua the Messiah, the Root and Offspring of David, will be married to the land of Israel, the people of Israel, and those who believe from all nations forever. This will be the fullness of the restoration of the cultivated Olive Tree. The Olive Tree does not and cannot exist in mid air, but its foundation is Yeshua through His covenant with Abraham, its first-fruits was David and Solomon's Kingdom, its fulfilment came through the death, burial and ressurection of

Jews, Arabs, and those from all nations worshiping the God of Israel-Yeshua with the heart of David will all be branches of the one 'Cultivated Olive Tree of Life.'

94

Yeshua, and its fullness will come through Yeshua's reign on David's throne on the Temple Mount forever.

The House, Heart, Tabernacle and Throne of David are being restored to prepare the way for the King of Glory to reign forever on the Temple Mount (Ezekiel 43:1-7), the place of the soles of His feet among the Israelites forever—on the Throne of David. The House and Tabernacle of David are being restored to prepare the way for Jews, Arabs, and those from all nations worldwide to worship the God of Israel-Yeshua with the heart of David in spirit and truth as part of the one 'Cultivated Olive Tree of Life.' This is the destiny for all those who make their choice to be rooted and grounded forever in and with Yeshua reigning on the Temple Mount and in the New Jerusalem that is coming down from Heaven.

The Olive Tree does not and can not exist in mid air, but its foundation is Yeshua through His covenant with Abraham, its first-fruits was David and Solomon's Kingdom, its fulfilment came through the death, burial and ressurrection of Yeshua, and its fullness will come through Yeshua's reign on David's throne on the Temple Mount forever.

PART IV

The Covenants and The Land

Chapter 10

The land and People of Israel to be Married to the Lord

Isaiah 62 is one of the fundamental scriptures for our 24-hour Watch. Because of your prayers, the God of Israel is beginning to root out replacement theology. In the last two years, there has been an incredible lifting of the veil over the largest churches of the world in terms of standing with Israel. They are beginning to recognize God's promise that the land belongs to Israel.

> **For Zion's sake I will not keep silent, for Jerusalem's sake I will not remain quiet, till her righteousness shines out like the dawn, her salvation like a blazing torch. The nations will see your righteousness, and all kings your glory; you will be called by a new name that the mouth of the LORD will bestow. You will be a crown of splendour in the LORD's hand, a royal diadem in the hand of your God. No longer will they call you Deserted, or name your land Desolate. But you will be called Hephzibah, and your land Beulah; for the LORD will take delight in you, and your land will be married. As a young man marries a maiden, so will your sons marry you; as a bridegroom rejoices over his bride, so will your God rejoice over you.**
>
> **I have posted watchmen on your walls, O Jerusalem; they will never be silent day or night.**

> **You who call on the LORD, give yourselves no rest, and give Him no rest till he establishes Jerusalem and makes her the praise of the earth.**
>
> **Pass through, pass through the gates! Prepare the way for the people. Build up, build up the highway! Remove the stones. Raise a banner for the nations (Isaiah 62:1-7,10).**

Reflect for a moment, if you haven't thought of it before, that in verse 4, **"No longer will they call you Deserted or your land Desolate** [deserted–this is describing the land of Israel]. **But you will be called Hephzibah, and your land Beulah; for the LORD will take delight in you and your land will be married ... to the LORD."** Proclaim and believe this scripture as you are standing as watchmen on the walls of Jerusalem in Jerusalem and all over the world—THE LAND OF ISRAEL IS TO BE MARRIED TO THE LORD. In the next verse it says—The people will also be married to the Lord, because as the bridegroom rejoices over the bride so will the Lord rejoice over you. God is not only married to the Church, but also he has made a marriage covenant with the Jewish people, the people of Israel. He has made a covenant to restore the land and people of Israel to the God of Israel. The Bible says the Promised Land is married to the Lord and we need to stand with the Lord that this land and the people will be married to the God of Israel and recognize that their land is married to the Lord.

Many people in Israel are ready to give up the land upon which the God of Israel made covenants with them because they

The Land of Israel is to be married to the Lord.

do not believe in the God of Israel, the God of their fathers, and do not believe in His covenants. Pray that the Jewish people will see God's covenants with them, and that they will not allow them to be hijacked and the people driven out of the land the God of Israel promised them. Pray this not only because the Lord is married to the people, to the Church worldwide, and to the Jewish people for their salvation, but also because the Lord is also married to the land.

Covenants were made in Shechem, Beth El, Hebron and Jerusalem. Because the Land belongs to Him, His covenants not only were made with regard to the people, but also with the land. Some say the Muslims and the nations are going to hijack the land. We need to say, "I am going to stand and pray that it will not be hijacked and that the people of this land will receive revelation."

Because of the failure of many to stand against the Crusades, the Inquisition, the Holocaust and other terrible misrepresentations of true Christianity throughout history, there are many Jewish atheists and agnostics in Israel and the nations who do not even believe in the God of Israel. As Christians, we are very sorry for these horrible crimes and ask the Jewish people to forgive

God called the Jewish people to stand for their inheritance.

us and rise in faithfulness to believe in the One True God of Israel who we believe in. We pray that the people who are believers will believe in God's covenants with the land. Even some Orthodox Jews don't believe in or stand for the covenants of God. We especially need to pray that God will bring a revelation of His covenants about His Land to ALL the Jewish people of Israel, because God called the Jewish people to stand for their inheritance.

While there have been some positive changes, we must also continue to pray for removal of the deception of replacement theology in the Christian Church, which says the Abrahamic Covenants are only for the Church and do not relate to the Land of Israel today. This is deception and a curse that must be repented for to relieve the Church and Nations from judgement and for God's blessing to be fully released and fully flow to Israel, the Church, and the Nations.

A kingdom or nation divided against itself cannot stand. As the Jewish covenantal people and Sons of Abraham in Israel and worldwide and Christians worldwide who believe in the God of Israel and His covenants with Abraham by faith, we all need to stand together as one as watchmen on the walls of Jerusalem. We must take no rest and give God no rest until Jerusalem is established as a praise in the earth, with Jew, Arab, Egypt, Israel, and Assyria all worshiping God together as a blessing in the midst of the earth. Amen!

"Son of man, prophesy to the mountains of Israel and say, 'O mountains of Israel, hear the word of the LORD. This is what the Sovereign LORD says: The enemy said of you, "Aha! The ancient heights have become our possession." ' Therefore prophesy and say, 'This is what the Sovereign LORD says: Because they ravaged and hounded you from every side so that you became the possession of the rest of the nations and the object of people's malicious talk and slander, therefore, O mountains of Israel, hear the word of the Sovereign LORD: This is what the Sovereign LORD says to the mountains and the hills, to the ravines and the valleys, to the desolate ruins and the deserted towns that have been plundered and ridiculed by the rest of the nations around you–this is what the Sovereign Lord says: In my burning zeal I have spoken against the rest of the nations, and against Edom, for with glee and with malice in their heart they made my land their own possession so that they might plunder its pasture-land.' Therefore prophesy concerning the land of Israel and say to the mountains and hills, to the ravines and valleys: 'This is what the Sovereign LORD says: I speak in my jealous wrath because you have suffered the scorn of the nations. Therefore this is what the Sovereign LORD says: I swear with uplifted hand that the nations around you will also suffer scorn.

"'But you, O mountains of Israel, will produce branches and fruit for my people Israel, for they will soon come home. I am concerned for you and will look on you with favour; you will be ploughed and sown, and I will multiply the number of people upon you, even the whole house of Israel. The towns will be inhabited and the ruins rebuilt (Ezekiel 36:1-10).'"

When the God of Israel prepared to bring the Jewish people out of Egypt He told Moses to proclaim to Pharaoh to "Let My people go that they may worship me [in their land]." Truly the reason for *Aliyah* (return of the Jewish people) to the whole land of Israel, especially to the places of covenants and covenant alters—Mount Hermon, Shechem, Beth El, Hebron, Jerusalem—is for the Jewish people to worship the God of Israel. According to the *Tanak,* the calling and destiny of the Jewish people is not just to worship God alone in their land in the midst of the Middle East, but the Holy Spirit through the prophet Isaiah said:

In that day there will be a highway from Egypt to Assyria. The Assyrians will go to Egypt and the Egyptians to Assyria. The Egyptians and Assyrians will worship together. In that day Israel will be the third, along with Egypt and Assyria, a blessing on the earth. The LORD Almighty will bless them, saying, "Blessed be Egypt my people, Assyria my handiwork, and Israel my inheritance" (Isaiah 19:23-25).

To conclude, Reuven, an Israeli leader, offers this prayer:

No eye has seen, no ear has heard, no mind has conceived what God has prepared for those who love Him (I Corinthians 2:9).

103

Father, we ask today in Messiah's name, that our eyes will be opened up even as the eyes of Abraham were opened up to see in the spirit those things that were impossible for man. A man who was barren, a wife who was barren and yet promised that his seed would be as the dust of the earth and as the stars of heaven and that he would become a father of a multitude of nations. He believed God and it was accounted to him as righteousness.

Father, in Messiah's name, we ask as sons of Abraham, Oh God, as we go into these end days, that the eyes of our spirits be opened up more and more to see the unfolding of the restoration of all things that were spoken by the prophets, Oh God, for the revelation of Messiah to come in all fullness to this earth; and Father we pray about the things that we heard this morning, things that are precious to You, things that are the pillars and the root and the foundations of our faith, ones that were laid by the living God himself.

Father, we receive the word that has been spoken today and Lord, we ask as You are raising up in this plan, a remnant out of the Jews, out of the Arabs, Oh God, sons who have received the spirit of adoption; and Lord, I pray as we heard Israel has in many ways fought with the inheritance, Lord God, through unbelief and often even despising the inheritance, Lord God, we ask Your forgiveness for that. We ask for Your forgiveness, Oh God, that we so often disdained the precious things of God and chose Babylon over Jerusalem. Lord we ask Your forgiveness, here, in the name of Messiah; and Lord, even in the Body of Messiah so many of those in the seed of Abraham, Isaac, and Jacob who have not seen these things and have not counted these things as being precious, Oh Lord, we ask forgiveness in Messiah's name.

Oh God, that the eyes of our spirits be opened more and more to see the unfolding of the restoration of all things.

Father, even as You have begun to establish a remnant who are sons, Lord, we do want to take ownership, in the name of Messiah, of the inheritance that You have given to us as Your people.

We stand in faith, Oh God, before You in faith over principalities and powers and that heaven and earth shall pass away but the word of God shall stand; and all things, oh God, that You preordained before the foundation of the world, Oh God, they shall be fulfilled; and Lord, our feet stand upon this ground as Your feet, Oh God, taking ownership of those things that are first of all Yours, Oh God, that are first of all Messiah's. This is Your land, Oh Lord, and You have made us stewards of God; and Lord, we accept that stewardship, in Messiah's name, for the Glory of God and for the coming forth of Your kingdom, Lord God. For You have chosen Israel and Jerusalem to be the center, to be the kingdom of God in this Earth that You have ordained according to Your will.

Lord, we accept the stewardship of this land, in Messiah's name, for your Glory.

We honor Your word Lord. We love Your word Lord. We submit ourselves to You, Oh God, and we ask, Oh God, for the spirit of revelation to begin to fall upon this land. We ask for the spirit of revelation to fall upon the people of Israel, Oh God, that the Holy Spirit will enlighten the hearts of the unbelievers, Oh God, even some of the Orthodox Jews who need to see the reality of Your word, to see the reality of Your covenant, and to see the reality of Your promises in regard to the land. That we would repent as a nation before You for our sins of unbelief and disobedience, Oh God, let that spirit of revelation come upon us in the nation of Israel especially during this time.

Lord, we do ask for the Arab believers. It must begin with them, Oh Lord. We pray, Oh God, that their hearts would be so in love with You, Lord, that they will just feel that they would not be fulfilled in their spirits until they enter into the fullness, until they understand what is in Your heart. This is not a political issue, Oh Lord. This is an issue of the mind of God, of the will of God, of the plan of God, and of the order of God. Only in God's order will the blessing of God fall upon the Arab people, Oh God; and by dishonoring that order they are depriving themselves of the blessing that You have. So we pray, Oh God, for the spirit of revelation to come upon our Arab brethren,

105

Lord God, that they would see by the spirit and that they would love the word of God and the covenants of God; that they would come into submission to this divine plan that You would release unto them the fullness of blessing, Oh God.

And we do pray for this whole area, the heartland of Israel—-Judea and Samaria. In this very area we pray for the settlers, Lord, we pray for the settlers. Many of them have faith in Your word, Oh God, and stand strong against the opposition of the Nations and Islam. We pray that You would begin to come upon them with Your Holy Spirit and that they would trust in you with all of their hearts. You said as the Jewish people will turn to the Lord they will be unveiled, that the veil would be removed as they turn to the Lord. Oh God, as they turn to You, the God of Reconciliation, we pray for the Arab villages in Judea and Samaria.

You are the God of the impossible. Pour out Your Spirit, Lord. Pour out Your mercy Lord God. Deliver them, Oh God, from the curses of Islam and from the blindness of Islam. Give Your redemption through the blood of the Passover Lamb. We proclaim the power of Your blood Messiah over these Arab villages and say, let redemption come in Messiah's name! We thank You Father. We thank You for the word that has been proclaimed today. May it be the confession of our faith before You this day, Oh God, that Your will be done on earth as it is in Heaven.

In Messiah's Name. Amen!!

Chapter 11

Adopting the Covenant Altars

Prayers at All Nations Convocation Jerusalem

In September 2002, representatives from the nations of the world adopted the altars.

Shechem Covenant Altar

Was adopted by nations from the three Northern Gates: Mount Carmel Gate, Damascus Gate, Pisgat Ze'ev Gate.

Beth El Covenant Altar

Was adopted by nations from the three Western Gates: Mevasseret Qiryat Jearim Gate, Jaffa Gate, New Gate.

Hebron Covenant Altar

Was adopted by nations from the three Southern Gates: Mount Zion Gate, Bethlehem Gate, Ein Kerem Gate.

Mt. Moriah (Jerusalem) Covenant Altar

Was adopted by nations from the three Eastern Gates: Lions Gate, Golden Gate, Bethany Gate.

The nation of Israel sealed the prayers.

SHECHEM ALTAR (Northern Gates)

UKRAINE, David Gregory:

Oh Holy Father, I say to You, Oh Lord, our God, our friend, our creator. You are the great 'I AM' and we thank You for enabling us to be here in the City of the Great King. You have called us together for such a time as this that the word goes out of Zion, out of Jerusalem and touches the ends of the Earth. And we thank You Lord for Shechem Altar and call forth everyone. You said You would pour out Your spirit over people in the day of Your power and we are here in Jerusalem and we call for 24-hour worship, we call forth intercession from the nations and we call forth Aliyah. Send prophets and send prophetic words that will shake everything that can be shaken and that which will remain, will remain.

Oh Lord God, touch the entire world, make Your people willing to obey Your power. Today is the day of salvation. Oh God, that Egypt, Israel, and Assyria will worship in the City of the Great King. Oh Lord God, we look forward to that. You are the same yesterday, today, and forever.

We ask for apostolic authority over Shechem, Lord God. We ask for signs and wonders. You will raise the dead, heal the sick, and heal the broken hearts. You will do greater things now, because You went to the Father.

Thank You, Lord, that You will reign upon this altar. We call forth every nation in these gates to see the SIGNIFICANCE OF THIS ALTAR IN THE HEAVENS and we speak peace to this place and to Israel. We love you Israel. Lord God save the multitudes, draw them to Your people through prophetic words, raise up churches everywhere.

In Messiah's name, Amen!

IRAQ, Yosef:

Lord we glorify Your Name. You are the beginning and the end, the first and the last. I thank You for Your blood and for Your will, that You will achieve all things. I call upon Your Name and announce the name of Messiah, the precious King over this altar, the name of the King of Kings, the One who created the earth and the heavens, the beginning and the end. Show the world who You are.

By the Name of Messiah I pray, Amen.

BETH EL ALTAR (Western Gates)

UK, Charles Abraham, Kensington Temple - the Largest Church in Western Europe:

Heavenly father, "If the foundations are destroyed, how can the righteous stand." We want to thank You for the foundations that Abraham laid. The foundation of that altar at Beth El. Years later You confirmed that You are most committed to that covenant because in that place You appeared again to Jacob. Father, You opened the heavens over him and You showed him the ladder that came out of heaven.

Father, this day we come to You and pray that from the gates of the west, we adopt this covenanted place called Beth El. We adopt this altar and we ask You, Father God, to open the windows of heaven, to cast down the ladder out of heaven to come down to us, to cause the angels to give revelation to us as they descend to this place. And we pray, even as we are almost caught up from that place, Lord, we pray that the supply of heaven to come to this gate. Lord, we pray for revelation knowledge to come through this gate. Lord, we adopt this gate in the Name of Messiah.

You are the God of Beth El, and we remember what You said to Jacob, "I will not leave you." Therefore we want to remind You that we stand with that covenant You made with Abraham and Jacob. And we know You will not leave us unless and until You fulfill all the promises You made.

LORD, REVIVE THE COVENANT OF THAT ALTAR. Let Your name be glorified; and I call the names of the west and say, "Beth El, Your altar, uphold it in spirit, worship around it, the glory of the Lord will descend upon us. We will see the glory of God and we

109

shall not leave the House of the Lord until all these things happen. We will exalt the name of the Lord from this altar through our gate. In Messiah's name."

All the nations of the gates of the west, say this to me, "Father, in the Name of Messiah, we adopt this altar of Beth El and we promise to intercede and worship unto Messiah on this throne." Amen!

GERMAN-SPEAKING NATIONS, Geri Keller:

Father we adopt this altar. Just as Jacob came to this place while running away from his brother, and brought back the stolen inheritance, we recognize that we are nations who stole the inheritance of other nations and we come back and bring back here to release the inheritance of others. We bring back the money, the relationships, and the treasures that are gifts of the German-speaking world. We will build up the altar. We call forth prophecy for the German-speaking nations.

Jacob laid his head on the stones here. Our Messiah said, "I have no place to lay my head," and I pray for those German-speaking nations that we will say, "LORD, HERE ARE OUR HEARTS, YOU CAN LAY DOWN HERE IN OUR HEARTS," and we will in the presence of the Holy Spirit in our nations make Your dwelling now, Lord. We ask for open heavens. We confess and confirm that we will together build this altar of Beth El again and again. Amen.

USA, Bobbie Byerly, World Prayer Center Colorado Springs, CO.:

Father we bow before You for Your wisdom, Your knowledge, Your revelation. We thank You because Your revelation has come to us and just as we adopt this altar, we also say as Jacob said, "Surely this is the gate of Heaven."

Father we call forth people across the Americas, across the United States of America. We pray that revelation will go right across our nation and that You will break through the replacement theology and people will come and they will acknowledge the God of Abraham.

We thank You Father and we say to the United States of America, "Stand strong to the God of Abraham, do not be deceived," and Father we speak grace to the United States of America at this hour of great decision and Father, Jacob was making a great decision when he saw the heavens open and the ladder came down from heaven. Lord, we cry out to You for the United States of America, please open their blind eyes and deaf ears. We believe that You will penetrate our churches, oh God of Israel, and we ask You to draw them to You, send them a prophetic word to come to this land so that they too will have revelation, that You will reveal Your beloved son, the Messiah; and Father we pray for all the Jews in America that they too will have a revelation of God in Messiah's name. Amen!

HEBRON ALTAR (Southern Gates)

ZIMBABWE, Langton Gatsi:

Father, we want to thank You for the revelations that You reveal to us all. We see how You showed us all to adopt the altars through our gates, Oh Lord. We are moving closer to our own adoption of Your age-old covenants. The things You spoke to Abraham continue to speak to many generations. I believe as seed of Abraham we have come to speak to those altars to remind You of Your blessings on Abraham on the altar of Hebron. And we pray that You will remove everything that wants to hinder. We ask You to sweep away the refuge of darkness so that the covenant of Abraham will continue to speak to our generation.

And this is why, Lord, we speak to You now and say, God, we speak to the altars that were raised by Your servant in Hebron when he was coming from Africa with the word that You gave him. He came to Hebron and this is what we want to say, Lord. We want to see that the altar he built will not fall to the ground but will be fulfilled because You are the God of Abraham, You made the covenant with him. We ask You O Covenant God of Israel, we remind You of every word that You spoke to Your servant and we as his seed and we as his people, because we are children of Abraham by faith and we want to see, Oh God, everything fulfilled.

This is why Lord we exalt You and we say, God, we adopt the altar of Hebron. We adopt it, Oh God, so that we will begin to reign just like David reigned for seven years. Father, we want to begin to reign, Oh God, with You, Messiah. We begin to possess, in the Name of Messiah, so that here is the foundation, Father, the fathers of our fathers are laid down here—Abraham, Isaac, and Jacob. Our fathers are speaking in that area so this is why we say, Everlasting One, as they begin to speak, we will reign there Lord, we want to relay the foundation. We want to see the foundation coming back into the Church. Father, as we are reminded of Hebron. We are reminded of what the fathers, the partakers of the covenant have done, Oh God, in the Name of Messiah. Lord we thank You because we are moving forward, we are getting closer to the very things that You wanted us to have Lord. So we give You the praise in the Name that is above every Name. Thank You Abba. Halleluyah.

TUNISIA, Mokhtar:

Lord, I thank You and glorify Your Name for You are the God of Israel, and You are the only one whose Name is glorified over everything else. You called Your people from Egypt. As the people of North Africa, we pray for an open highway to Israel. We pray that through this highway, people will come to worship You and to glorify Your Name. God, we the people of Egypt and the Arab countries glorify Your Name because You chose us to be Your children too. You love us and Your love for us is so big. I really pray that You will make them all one soul and one heart for You.

You are the Light. We pray that You will give us Your light. We pray from our hearts that You will give us this adoption so that Your Name will be glorified everywhere.

I pray this in the Name of the Father, the Son, and the Holy Spirit. Amen!

MOUNT MORIAH/JERUSALEM ALTAR (Eastern Gates)

CHINA, Leader of Underground Church (almost 100 million Christians in China):

We thank You and praise You, Lord. We dedicate to You the nations from the Golden Gate. We pray from this direction (east). We pray that You will raise hundreds and thousands of prayer warriors and also raise many 24-hour prayer watches so that many souls can be saved. We pray that You will destroy the power of idols.

In this direction we pray that many Jews can come back to the ways of their God. We pray Lord that You will provide many people to help them to make Aliyah. Lord, we thank You.

We will make every effort to protect and guard this altar in prayer and keep the 24-hour watch over this altar. We shall prepare the way and welcome the coming King.

With all glory and honor to Messiah, we pray in His Name. Amen.

TAIWAN, Jonathan Tseng, Ling Liang—Largest Church in Taiwan:

We shall restore the altar of Jerusalem. May You release fire from Heaven to burn and purify the nations and the Church. May You fill us with Your mighty power that we shall depend on Your Name to do Your work. We dedicate our lives to You once again; and we shall come to Jerusalem to watch this altar, watch over Your temple.

We look upon You and we offer our lives to You. We pray for all the nations in this direction. We pray that praise and worship shall be raised as burnt offerings to You. We will prepare the way for You and give all the glory to You. May we give our love and may the blood of the Messiah strengthen the covenant that He made with us. May You encourage us and give us the anointing in praise and worship so we can come to You 24 hours. May we become a Church of worship and praise. May the fire from heaven burn among the Church until the day You come. We thank You for the covenant of Abraham.

We praise You and honor You forever and ever. Amen.

113

INDIA, Thomas George, Pastor of the largest Church in India:

Father God, we praise You as we pray for the Golden Gate nations, for their adoption of this altar. Our father Abraham lived in temporary tents, but built permanent altars. He pitched tents, but it was permanent altars, Oh God. Just as the permanent Moriah Altar was raised, TRUE WORSHIP WAS OFFERED TO YOU WHEN OUR FOREFATHER LAID AT THE ALTAR THE BEST OF HIS HEART FOR YOU. Even at Your provision, when the true worship rules at the moment, let true intercession and true worship rise from the heart of the nations.

Father, we pray for Jerusalem, the altar at Mount Moriah. We prepare for the Great King to come. We pray that everything becomes temporary and the altars become permanent and anything that comes as a hindrance will be destroyed. Let this true worship arise in thy presence and let the people worship in true spirit. We thank You Lord that You will raise the people to come and offer true worship. Draw the nations to own this altar and raise up offerings of true worship to the Messiah, the great King.

In Messiah's Name, Amen.

THE SEAL

ISRAEL, Reuven:

Father God, I thank You for every prayer that has gone up and every prayer that will go up as a result of this revelation You are granting the nations at this time, through the Spirit, to lay hold of the realities of these altars and what they signify and what You want to release in the restoration of these realities in our time; and Lord, we do confess that we need all the support for the present time, that You will give the revelation of the word; and I want to seal every prayer that has been prayed here. Father, that it will bring much fruit to all of these nations, Lord God, in relation to these four altars that we have just been praying about. Father, we seal these prayers and we say, may each one of these brethren here be ambassadors in the Spirit to their nations and to their continents, Lord, in relation to these four altars, in the Name of Messiah. Father, at the same time, as these altars relate so very specifically to Your promise to the nation of Israel, to the promise that You gave to Israel in relation to the land of Israel, Lord, at a time when this whole reality is being challenged by all the nations of the world and even Israel herself, as there have been Israeli governments that were willing to compromise, give up, Oh God, and despise their inheritance of the Lord.

Father, we pray that as Israelis, we would not be ashamed of the inheritance of your house given us; that we would not quickly give it away for a bowl of lentil soup, Lord God. Lord, that we would take possession as sons in the Messiah in the spirit of those things that You have committed to the nation of Israel through the covenants.

Lord God, we accept that we are connected to these altars, that our fathers have made. Oh God, we pray that You will give a revelation to Israel that we would be able to stand in the priesthood, that You committed to us at this time Father, and as we would do that, Lord God, we pray for greater revelation for the nation of Israel that we, Oh God, will cherish that which has been granted to us by God, for Lord it is through this land that You want to take possession of the planet. It is through this city that You want Your kingdom to come to all the Earth.

So we pray, Lord, for Israel that we would take ownership of these altars in relation to Your covenant with Israel and ultimately their call to the nations of the world. So we stand together here today as representatives from Israel and the nations adopting and confirming these altars that have been established by our fathers, Lord God.

In the Name of Messiah, Amen!!!

Chapter 12

Six Hundred Scripture References to God's Covenants and the Land of Israel

To read, pray, and meditate on about God's covenants with the land of Israel

Genesis 12:2, 3 I will make you [Abram] into a great nation and I will bless you; I will make your name great, and you will be a blessing. I will bless those who bless you, and whoever curses you I will curse; and all peoples on earth will be blessed through you.

Genesis 12:6, 7 Abram traveled through the land as far as the site of the great tree of Moreh at Shechem. At that time the Canaanites were in the land. The LORD appeared to Abram and said, "To your offspring I will give this land." So he built an altar there to the LORD who had appeared to him.

Genesis 12:8 From there [Shechem] he [Abram] went on towards the hills east of Bethel and pitched his tent, with Bethel on the west and Ai on the east. There he built an altar to the LORD and he called on the name of the LORD.

Genesis 13:14-18 The LORD said to Abram after Lot had departed from him, "Lift up your eyes from where you are and look north and south, east and west. All the land that you see I will give to you and your offspring for ever. I will make your offspring like the dust of the earth, so that if anyone could count the dust, then your offspring could be counted. Go, walk through the length and breadth of the land, for I am giving it to you."

So Abram moved his tents and went to live near the great trees of Mamre at Hebron, where he built an altar to the LORD.

Genesis 14:18-20 Then Melchizedek king of Salem brought out bread and wine. He was priest of God Most High, and he blessed Abram, saying, "Blessed be Abram by God Most High, Creator of heaven and earth. And blessed be God Most High, who delivered your enemies into your hand." Then Abram gave him a tenth of everything.

Genesis 15:5-7 He took him outside and said, "Look up at the heavens and count the stars—if indeed you can count them." Then he said to him, "So shall your offspring be."

Abram believed the LORD, and he credited it to him as righteousness.

He also said to him, "I am the LORD, who brought you out of Ur of the Chaldeans to give you this land to take possession of it."

Genesis 15:9-21 So the LORD said to him, "Bring me a heifer, a goat and a ram, each three years old, along with a dove and a young pigeon."

Abram brought all these to him, cut them in two and arranged the halves opposite each other; the birds, however, he did not cut in half. Then birds of prey came down on the carcasses, but Abram drove them away.

As the sun was setting, Abram fell into a deep sleep, and a thick and dreadful darkness came over him. Then the LORD said to him, "Know for certain that your descendants will be strangers in a country not their own, and they will be enslaved and ill-treated four hundred years. But I will punish the nation they serve as slaves, and afterwards they will come out with great possessions. You, however, will go to your fathers in peace and be buried at a good old age. In the fourth generation your descendants will come back here, for the sin of the Amorites has not yet reached its full measure."

When the sun had set and darkness had fallen, a smoking brazier [oven] with a blazing torch appeared and passed between the pieces. On that day the LORD made a covenant with Abram and said, "To your descendants I give this land, from the river of Egypt to the great river, the Euphrates—the land of the Kenites, Kenizzites, Kadmonites, Hittites, Perizzites, Rephaites, Amorites, Canaanites, Girgashites and Jebusites."

Genesis 17:2 I will confirm my covenant between me and you and will greatly increase your numbers.

Genesis 17:4, 5 "As for me, this is my covenant with you: You will be the father of many nations. No longer will you be called Abram; your name will be Abraham, for I have made you a father of many nations.

Genesis 17:7, 8 I will establish my covenant as an everlasting covenant between me and you and your descendants after you for the generations to come, to be your God and the God of your descendants after you. The whole land of Canaan, where you are now an alien, I will give as an everlasting possession to you and your descendants after you; and I will be their God.

Genesis 17:10 This is my covenant with you and your descendants after you, the covenant that you are to keep: Every male among you shall be circumcised.

Genesis 17:13 Whether born in your household or bought with your money, they must be circumcised. My covenant in your flesh is to be an everlasting covenant.

Genesis 17:18, 19 And Abraham said to God, "If only Ishmael might live under your blessing!" Then God said, "Yes [No in NKJV], but your wife Sarah will bear you a son, and you will call him Isaac. I will establish my covenant with him as an everlasting covenant for his descendants after him."

Genesis 17:21 But my covenant I will establish with Isaac, whom Sarah will bear to you by this time next year.

Genesis 18:1, 2 The LORD appeared to Abraham near the great trees of Mamre while he was sitting at the entrance of his tent in the heat of the day. Abraham looked up and saw three men standing nearby. When he saw them, he hurried from the entrance of his tent to meet them and bowed low to the ground.

Genesis 22:2 Then God said, "Take your son, your only son, Isaac, whom you love, and go to the region of Moriah. Sacrifice him there as a burnt offering on one of the mountains I will tell you about."

Genesis 22:8-14 Abraham answered, "God himself will provide the lamb for the burnt offering, my son." And the two of them went together.

When they reached the place God had told him about, Abraham built an altar there and arranged the wood on it. He bound his son Isaac and laid him on the altar, on top of the wood. Then he reached out his hand and took the knife to slay his son. But the angel of the LORD called out to him from heaven, "Abraham! Abraham!"

"Here I am," he replied.

"Do not lay a hand on the boy," he said. "Do not do anything to him. Now I know that you fear God, because you have not withheld from me your son, your only son."

Abraham looked up and there in a thicket he saw a ram caught by its horns. He went over and took the ram and sacrificed it as a burnt offering instead of his son. So Abraham called that place The LORD Will Provide. And to this day it is said, "On the mountain of the LORD it will be provided."

Genesis 23:17-20 So Ephron's field in Machpelah near Mamre [Hebron]—both the field and the cave in it, and all the trees within the borders of the field—was legally made over to Abraham as his property in the presence of all the Hittites who had come to the gate of the city. Afterwards Abraham buried his wife Sarah in the cave in the field of Machpelah near Mamre (which is at Hebron) in the land of Canaan. So the field and the cave in it were legally made over to Abraham by the Hittites as a burial site.

Genesis 25:9, 10 His sons Isaac and Ishmael buried him in the cave of Machpelah near Mamre, in the field of Ephron son of Zohar the Hittite, the field Abraham had bought from the Hittites. There, Abraham was buried with his Sarah.

Genesis 26:3, 4 Stay in this land for a while, and I will be with you and will bless you. For to you and your descendants I will give these lands and will confirm the oath I swore to your father Abraham. I will make your descendants as numerous as the stars in the sky and will give them all these lands, and through your offspring all nations on earth will be blessed.

Genesis 28:4 May he [God Almighty] give you [Jacob] and your descendants the blessing given to Abraham, so that you may take possession of the land where you now live as an alien, the land God gave to Abraham.

Genesis 28:10-17 Jacob left Beersheba and set out for Haran. When he reached a certain place, he stopped for the night because the sun had set. Taking one of the stones there, he put it under his head and lay down to sleep. He had a dream in which he saw a stairway resting on the earth, with its top reaching to heaven, and the angels of God were ascending and descending on it. There above it stood the LORD, and he said: "I am the LORD, the God of your father Abraham and the God of Isaac. I will give you and your descendants the land on which you are lying. Your descendants will be like the dust of the earth, and you will spread out to the west and to the east, to the north and to the south. All the peoples on earth will be blessed through you and your offspring. I am with you and will watch over you wherever you go, and I will bring you back to this land. I will not leave you until I have done what I have promised you."

When Jacob awoke from his sleep, he thought, "Surely the LORD is in this place, and I was not aware of it." He was afraid and said, "How awesome is this place! This is none other than the house of God [*Beth El*]; this is the gate of heaven."

Genesis 28:18-22 Early the next morning Jacob took the stone he had placed under his head and he set it up as a pillar and poured oil on top of it. He called that place *Beth El* [House of God], though the city used to be called Luz.

Then Jacob made a vow, saying, "If God will be with me and will watch over me on this journey I am taking and will give me food to eat and clothes to wear so that I return safely to my father's house, then the LORD will be my God and this stone that I have set up as a pillar will be God's house, and of all that you give me I will give you a tenth."

Genesis 31:13 I am the God of Bethel, where you anointed a pillar and where you made a vow to me. Now leave this land [Paddan Aram] at once and go back to your native land [Canaan].

Genesis 33:18 After Jacob came from Paddan Aram, he arrived safely at the city of Shechem in Canaan and camped within sight of the city. For a hundred pieces of silver, he bought from the sons of Hamor, the father of Shechem, the plot of ground where he pitched his tent. There he set up an altar and called it *El Elohe Israel* [God the God of Israel].

Genesis 35:9-12 After Jacob returned from Paddan Aram, God appeared to him again and blessed him. God said to him, "Your name is Jacob, but you will no longer be called Jacob; your name will be Israel." So He named him Israel. And God said to him, "I am God Almighty; be fruitful and increase in number. A nation and a community of nations will come from you, and kings will come from your body. The land I gave to Abraham and Isaac I also give you, and I will give this land to your descendants after you."

Genesis 48:3, 4 Jacob said to Joseph, "God Almighty appeared to me at Luz in the land of Canaan, and there he blessed me and said to me, 'I am going to make you fruitful and will increase your numbers. I will make you a community of peoples, and I will give this land as an everlasting possession to your descendants after you.' "

Genesis *48:22* And to you [Joseph], as one who is over your brothers, I [Jacob] give the ridge of the land I took from the Amorites [Shechem] with my sword and bow.

Genesis *49:29-32* Bury me [Jacob] with my fathers in the cave in the field of Ephron the Hittite, the cave in the field of Machpelah, near Mamre in Canaan [Hebron], which Abraham bought from Ephron the Hittite, along with the field. There Abraham and his wife Sarah were buried, there Isaac and his wife Rebekah were buried, and there I buried Leah. The field and the cave in it were bought from the Hittites.

Genesis *50:12, 13* So Jacob's sons did as he commanded them: They carried him to the land of Canaan and buried him in the cave in the field of Machpelah, near Mamre [Hebron], which Abraham had bought as a burial place from Ephron the Hittite, along with the field.

Genesis *50:24* Then Joseph said to his brothers, "I am about to die. But God will surely come to your aid and take you up out of this land to the land he promised on oath to Abraham, Isaac and Jacob."

Exodus *2:24* God heard their groaning and he remembered his covenant with Abraham, with Isaac and with Jacob.

Exodus *6:4, 5* I also established my covenant with them [Abraham, Isaac, and Jacob] to give them the land of Canaan, where they lived as aliens. Moreover, I have heard the groaning of the Israelites, whom the Egyptians are enslaving, and I have remembered my covenant.

Exodus *6:8* And I will bring you to the land I swore with uplifted hand to give to Abraham, to Isaac and to Jacob. I will give it to you as a possession. I am the LORD.

Exodus *12:25* When you enter the land that the LORD will give you as he promised, and observe this ceremony [Passover].

Exodus 19:4-6 "You yourselves have seen what I did to Egypt, and how I carried you on eagles' wings and brought you to myself. Now if you obey me fully and keep my covenant, then out of all nations you will be my treasured possession. Although the whole earth is mine, you will be for me a kingdom of priests and a holy nation." These are the words you are to speak to the Israelites.

Exodus 23:31 I will establish your borders from the Red Sea to the Sea of the Philistines, and from the desert to the River [the Euphrates].

Exodus 32:13 Remember your servants Abraham, Isaac and Israel, to whom you swore by your own self: "I will make your descendants as numerous as the stars in the sky and I will give your descendants all this land I promised them, and it will be their inheritance for ever."

Exodus 33:1 Then the LORD said to Moses, "Leave this place, you and the people you brought up out of Egypt, and go up to the land I promised on oath to Abraham, Isaac and Jacob, saying, "I will give it to your descendants."

Leviticus 20:24 But I said to you, "You will possess their land; I will give it to you as an inheritance, a land flowing with milk and honey." I am the LORD your God, who has set you apart from the nations.

Leviticus 25:2 When you enter the land that I am going to give to you, the land itself must observe a Sabbath to the LORD.

Leviticus 25:8-17 Count off seven Sabbaths of years—seven times seven years—so that the seven Sabbaths of years amount to a period of forty-nine years. Then have the trumpet sounded everywhere on the tenth day of the seventh month; on the Day of Atonement sound the trumpet throughout the land. Consecrate the fiftieth year and proclaim liberty throughout the land to all its inhabitants. It shall be a jubilee for you; each one for you is to return to his family property and each one to his own clan. The fiftieth year shall be a jubilee for you;

do not sow and do to reap what grows of itself or harvest the untended vines. For it is a jubilee and is to be holy for you; eat only what is taken directly from the fields.

In this Year of Jubilee everyone is to return to his own property.

If you sell land to one of your countrymen or buy any from him, do not take advantage of each other. You are to buy from your countryman on the basis of the number of years since the Jubilee. And he is to sell to you on the basis of the number of years left for harvesting crops. When the years are many, you are to increase the price, and when the year are few, you are to decrease the price, because what he is really selling you is the number of crops. Do not take advantage of each other, but fear your God. I am the LORD your God.

Leviticus 25:23-25 The land must not be sold permanently, because the land is mine and you are but aliens and tenants. Throughout the country that you hold as a possession, you must provide for the redemption of the land. If one of your countrymen becomes poor and sells some of his property, his nearest relative is to come and redeem what his countryman has sold.

Leviticus 25:38 I am the LORD your God, who brought you out of Egypt to give you the land of Canaan and to be your God.

Leviticus 26:9 I will look on you with favor and make you fruitful and increase your numbers, and I will keep my covenant with you.

Leviticus 26:42 I will remember my covenant with Jacob and my covenant with Isaac and my covenant with Abraham, and I will remember the land.

Leviticus 26:44, 45 Yet in spite of this, when they [Israel] are in the land of their enemies, I will not reject them or abhor them so as destroy to them completely, breaking my covenant with them. I am the LORD their God. But for their sake I will remember the covenant of their

125

ancestors, whom I brought out of Egypt in the sight of the nations to be their God. I am the LORD.

Numbers 10:29 We are setting out for the place about which the LORD said, "I will give you."

Numbers 11:12 Did I conceive all these people? Did I give them birth? Why do you tell me to carry them in my arms, as a nurse carries an infant, to the land you promised on oath to their forefathers?

Numbers 13:26, 30-32 They came back to Moses and Aaron and with whole Israelite community at Kadesh in the Desert of Paran. There they reported to them and to the whole assembly and showed the fruit of the land.

Then Caleb silenced the people before Moses and said, "We should go up and take possession of the land, for we can certainly do it."

But the men who had gone up with him said, "We can't attack those people, they are stronger than we are." And they spread among the Israelites a bad report about the land they had explored.

Numbers 14:7-9 And [Caleb] said to the entire Israelite assembly, "The land we passed through and explored is exceedingly good. If the LORD is pleased with us, he will lead us into the land, a land flowing with milk and honey, and will give it to us. Only do not rebel against the LORD. And do not be afraid of the people of the land, because we will swallow them up. Their protection is gone, but the LORD is with us. Do not be afraid of them.

Numbers 26:52-56 The LORD said to Moses, "The land is to be allotted to them as an inheritance based on the number of names. To a larger group give a larger inheritance, and to a smaller group a smaller one; each is to receive its inheritance according to the number of those listed. Be sure that the land is distributed by lot. What each group inherits will be according to the names for its ancestral tribe. Each inheritance is to be distributed by lot among the larger and smaller groups."

Numbers 27:12 Go up to the mountain in the Abarim Range and see the land I have given the Israelites.

Numbers 32:22 And this land will be your possession before the LORD

Numbers 36:7-9 No inheritance in Israel is to pass from tribe to tribe, for every Israelite shall keep the tribal land inherited from his forefathers. Every daughter who inherits land in any Israelite tribe must marry someone in her father's tribal clan, so that every Israelite will possess the inheritance of his fathers.

Deuteronomy 1:8 See, I have given you this land. Go and take possession of the land that the LORD swore he would give to your fathers—Abraham, Isaac and Jacob—and to their descendants after them.

Deuteronomy 1:21 See, the LORD your God has given you the land. Go up and take possession of it as the LORD, the God of your fathers, told you. Do not be afraid; do not be discouraged.

Deuteronomy 1:25 Taking with them some of the fruit of the land, they brought it down to us and reported, "It is a good land that the LORD our God is giving us."

Deuteronomy 1:38, 39 Joshua son of Nun, will enter it. Encourage him, because he will lead Israel to inherit it. …they will enter the land. I will give it to them and they will take possession of it.

Deuteronomy 3:28 …he will lead this people across and will cause them to inherit the land that you will see.

Deuteronomy 4:1 Follow them [decrees] so that you may live and may go in and take possession of the land that the LORD, the God of your fathers, is giving you.

Deuteronomy 4:14 …the land that you are crossing the Jordan to possess.

Deuteronomy 4:31 For the LORD your God is a merciful God; he will not abandon or destroy you or forget the covenant with your forefathers, which he confirmed to them by oath.

Deuteronomy 6:3 Hear, O Israel, and be careful to obey so that it may go well with you and that you may increase greatly in a land flowing with milk and honey, just as the LORD, the God of your fathers, promised you.

Deuteronomy 6:10, 11 When the LORD your God brings you into the land he swore to your fathers, to Abraham, Isaac, and Jacob, to give you—

Deuteronomy 6:18 Do what is right and good in the LORD's sight, so that it may go well with you and you may go in and take over the good land that the LORD promised on oath to your forefathers.

Deuteronomy 6:23 But he brought us out from there to bring us in and give us the land that he promised on oath to our forefathers.

Deuteronomy 7:9 Know therefore that the LORD your God is God; he is the faithful God, keeping his covenant of love to a thousand generations of those who love him and keep his commandments.

Deuteronomy 7:12, 13 If you pay attention to these laws and are careful to follow them, then the LORD your God will keep his covenant of love with you as he swore to your forefathers. He will bless the fruit of your womb, the crops of your land—your grain, new wine and oil—the calves of your herds and the lambs of your flocks in the land that he swore to your forefathers to give you.

Deuteronomy 8:1 Be careful to follow every command I am giving you today, so that you may live and increase and may enter and possess the land that the LORD promised on oath to your forefathers.

Deuteronomy 8:10 …praise the LORD your God for the good land he has given you.

Deuteronomy 8:18 But remember the LORD your God, for it is he who gives you the ability to produce wealth, and so confirms his covenant, which he swore.

Deuteronomy 10:11 "Go," the LORD said to me, "and lead the people on their way, so that they may enter and possess the land that I swore to their fathers to give them."

Deuteronomy 11:8, 9 …the land that you are crossing the Jordan to possess…the land that the LORD swore to your forefathers to give to them and their descendants, a land flowing with milk and honey.

Deuteronomy 11:21 So that your days may be many in the land that the LORD swore to give to your forefathers, as many as the days that the heavens are above the earth.

Deuteronomy 11:24 Your territory will extend from the desert to Lebanon, and from the Euphrates River to the western sea.

Deuteronomy 11:31 You are about to cross the Jordan to enter and take possession of the land the LORD your God is giving you.

Deuteronomy 15:4 There should be no poor among you, for in the land the LORD your God is giving you to possess as your inheritance, he will richly bless you.

Deuteronomy 16:20 Follow justice and justice alone, so that you may live and possess the land the LORD your God is giving you.

Deuteronomy 17:14 When you enter the land that the LORD your God is giving you and have taken possession of it and settle in it,…

Deuteronomy 18:9 When you enter the land the LORD your God is giving you, …

Deuteronomy 26:1, 2 When you have entered the land that the LORD your God is giving you as an inheritance and have taken possession of it and settled in it, take some of the first fruits of all that you produce from the soil of the land that the LORD your God is giving you and put them in a basket.

Deuteronomy 26:15 Look down from heaven, your holy dwelling-place, and bless your people Israel and the land you have given us as you promised on oath to our forefathers, a land flowing with milk and honey.

Deuteronomy 27:2, 3 When you have crossed the Jordan into the land the LORD your God is giving you, set up some large stones and coat them with plaster. Write on them all the words of this law when you have crossed the Jordan into the land the LORD your God is giving you, a land flowing with milk and honey, just as the LORD, the God of your fathers promised you.

Deuteronomy 27:4-6 And when you have crossed the Jordan, set up these stones on Mount Ebal, as I commanded you today, and coat them with plaster. Build there an altar to the LORD your God, an altar of stones. Do not use any iron tool upon them. Build the altar of the LORD your God with stones from the field and offer burnt offerings on it to the LORD your God.

Deuteronomy 27:12, 13 When you have crossed the Jordan, these tribes shall stand on Mount Gerizim to bless the people: Simeon, Levi, Judah, Issachar, Joseph and Benjamin. And these tribes shall stand on Mount Ebal to pronounce curses: Reuben, Gad, Asher, Zebulun, Dan and Naphtali.

Deuteronomy 28:8-11 The LORD your God will bless you in the land he is giving you. The LORD will establish you as his holy people, as he promised on oath, if you keep the commands of the LORD your God and walk in his ways. Then all the peoples on earth will see that you are called by the name of the LORD, and they will fear you. The LORD will grant you abundant prosperity—in the fruit of your womb, the young of your livestock and the crops of your ground—in the land he swore to your forefathers to give you.

Deuteronomy 30:5 He will bring you to the land that belonged to your fathers, and you will take possession of it. He will make you more prosperous and numerous than your fathers.

Deuteronomy 30:16-18 For I command you today to love the LORD your God, to walk in his ways, and to keep his commands, decrees and laws; then you will live and increase, and the LORD your God will bless you in the land you are entering to possess.

But if your heart turns away and you are not obedient, and if you are drawn away to bow down to other gods and worship them, I declare to you this day that you will certainly be destroyed. You will not live long in the land you are crossing the Jordan to enter and possess.

Deuteronomy 30:20 For the LORD is your life, and he will give you many years in the land he swore to give to your fathers, Abraham, Isaac and Jacob.

Deuteronomy 31:7 Then Moses summoned Joshua and said to him in the presence of all Israel, "Be strong and courageous, for you must go with this people into the land that the LORD swore to their forefathers to give them, and you must divide it among them as their inheritance."

Deuteronomy 31:13 Their children, who do not know this law, must hear it and learn to fear the LORD your God as long as you live in the land you are crossing the Jordan to possess.

Deuteronomy 31:20 When I have brought them into the land flowing with milk and honey, the land I promised on oath to their forefathers, and when they eat their fill and thrive, they will turn to other gods and worship them, rejecting me and breaking my covenant.

Deuteronomy 31:23 The LORD gave this command to Joshua son of Nun: "Be strong and courageous, for you will bring the Israelites into the land I promised them on oath, and I myself will be with you."

Deuteronomy 32:48, 49, 52 On the same day the LORD told Moses, "Go up into the Abarim Range to Mount Nebo in Moab, across from Jericho, and view Canaan, the land I am giving the Israelites as their own possession. Therefore, you will see the land only from a distance; you will not enter the land I am giving to the people of Israel."

Deuteronomy 33:13-16 May the LORD bless his land with the precious dew from heaven above and with the deep waters that lie below; with the best the sun brings forth and the finest the moon can yield; with the choicest gifts of the ancient mountains and the fruitfulness of the everlasting hills; with the best gifts of the earth and its fullness and the favour of him who dwelt in the burning bush.

Deuteronomy 34:1-4 Then Moses climbed Mount Nebo from the plains of Moab to the top of Pisgah, across from Jericho. There the LORD showed him the whole land—from Gilead to Dan, all of Naphtali, the territory of Ephraim and Manasseh, all the land of Judah as far as the western sea, the Negev and the whole region from the Valley of Jericho, the City of Palms, as far as Zoar. Then the LORD said to him: This is the land I promised on oath to Abraham, Isaac and Jacob when I said, "I will give it to your descendants."

Joshua 8:30-35 Then Joshua built on Mount Ebal an altar to the LORD, the God of Israel, as Moses the servant of the LORD had commanded the Israelites. He built it according to what is written in the Book of the Law of Moses—an altar of uncut stones, on which no iron tool had been used. On it they offered to the LORD burnt offerings and sacrificed fellowship offerings. There, in the presence of the Israelites, Joshua copied on stones the law of Moses, which he had written. All Israel, aliens and citizens alike, with their elders, officials and judges, were standing on both sides of the ark of the covenant of the LORD, facing those who carried it—the priests, who were Levites. Half of the people stood in front of Mount Gerizim and half of them in front of Mount Ebal [in Shechem], as Moses the servant of the LORD had formerly commanded when he gave instruction to bless the people of Israel.

Afterwards, Joshua read all the words of the law—the blessings and the curses—just as it is written in the Book of the Law. There was not a word of all that Moses had commanded that Joshua did not read to the whole assembly of Israel, including the women and children, and the aliens who lived among them.

Joshua 1:1-11 After the death of Moses the servant of the LORD, the LORD said to Joshua son of Nun, Moses' assistant: " Moses my servant is dead. Now then, you and all these people, get ready to cross the Jordan River into the land I am about to give to them—to the Israelites. I will give you every place where you set your foot, as I promised Moses. Your territory will extend from the desert to Lebanon, and from the great river, the Euphrates—all the Hittite country—to the Great Sea on the west. No-one will be able to stand up against you all the days of your life. As I was with Moses, so I will be with you; I will never leave you nor forsake you.

"Be strong and courageous, because you will lead these people to inherit the land I swore to their forefathers to give them. Be strong and very courageous. Be careful to obey all the law my servant Moses gave you; do not turn from it to the right or to the left, that you may be successful wherever you go. Do not let this Book of the Law depart from your mouth; meditate on it day and night, so that you may be careful to do everything written in it. Then you will be prosperous and successful. Have I not commanded you? Be strong and courageous. Do not be terrified; do not be discouraged, for the LORD your God will be with you wherever you go."

So Joshua ordered the officers of the people: "Go through the camp and tell the people: 'Get your supplies ready. Three days from now you will cross the Jordan here to get in and take possession of the land the LORD your God is giving you for your own.' "

Joshua 11:16, 17 So Joshua took this entire land: the hill country, all the Negev, the whole region of Goshen, the western foothills, the

Arabah and the mountains of Israel with their foothills, from Mount Halak, which rises towards Seir, to Baal Gad in the Valley of Lebanon below Mount Hermon.

Joshua 11:23 So Joshua took the entire land, just as the LORD had directed Moses, and he gave it as an inheritance to Israel according to their tribal divisions.

Joshua 14:1-5 Now these are the areas the Israelites received as an inheritance in the land of Canaan, which Eleazar the priest, Joshua son of Nun and the heads of the tribal clans of Israel allotted to them. Their inheritances were assigned by lot to the nine-and-a-half tribes, as the LORD had commanded through Moses. Moses had granted the two-and-a-half tribes their inheritances east of the Jordan but had not granted the Levites an inheritance among the rest, for the sons of Joseph had become two tribes—Manasseh and Ephraim. The Levites received no share of the land but only towns to live in, with pasture-lands for their flocks and herds. So the Israelites divided the land, just as the LORD had commanded Moses.

Joshua 14:7-9 I was forty years old when Moses the servant of the LORD sent me from Kadesh Barnea to explore the land. And I brought him back a report according to my convictions, but my brothers who went up with me made the hearts of the people sink. I, however, followed the LORD my God wholeheartedly. So on that day Moses swore to me, "The land on which your feet have walked will be your inheritance and that of your children for ever, because you have followed the Lord my God wholeheartedly."

Joshua 14:13-15 Then Joshua blessed Caleb son of Jephunneh and gave him Hebron as his inheritance. So Hebron has belonged to Caleb son of Jephunneh the Kenizzite ever since, because he followed the LORD the God of Israel, wholeheartedly. (Hebron used to be called Kiriath Arba after Arba, who was the greatest man among the Anakites.)

Joshua 15:13 In accordance with the LORD's command to him Joshua gave to Caleb son of Jephunneh a portion in Judah—Kiriath Arba, that is, Hebron.

Joshua 15, 16,17,18, and 19 Description of land Joshua leads Israel to conquor.

Joshua 18:21, 22, 28 The tribe of Benjamin, clan by clan, had the following cities: ... Bethel...This was the inheritance of Benjamin for its clans.

Joshua 20:7 So they [Israelites] set apart [as a city of refuge] Kedesh in Galilee in the hill country of Naphtali, Shechem in the hill country of Ephraim, and Kiriath Arba (that is Hebron) in the hill country of Judah.

Joshua 21:9-12 From the tribes of Judah and Simeon they allotted the following towns by name (these towns were assigned to the descendants of Aaron who were from the Kohathite clans of the Levites, because the first lot fell to them): They gave them Kiriath Arba (that is, Hebron), with its surrounding pasture-land, in the hill country of Judah. (Arba was the forefather of Anak.) But the fields and villages around the city they had given to Caleb son of Jephunneh as his possession. So to the descendants of Aaron the priest they gave Hebron (a city of refuge for one accused of murder),......

Joshua 21:20, 21 The rest of the Kohathite clans of the Levites were allotted towns from the tribe of Ephraim: In the hill country of Ephraim they were given Shechem (a city of refuge for one accused of murder).

Joshua 24:1-27 Then Joshua assembled all the tribes of Israel at Shechem. He summoned the elders, leaders, judges and officials of Israel, and they presented themselves before God.

Joshua said to all the people, "This is what the LORD, the God of Israel, says: 'Long ago your forefathers, including Terah the father of Abraham and Nahor, lived beyond the River and worshipped other gods. But I took your father Abraham from the land beyond the River and led him throughout Canaan and gave him many descendants. I

135

gave him Isaac, and to Isaac I gave Jacob and Esau. I assigned the hill country of Seir to Esau, but Jacob and his sons went down to Egypt.

"'Then I sent Moses and Aaron, and I afflicted the Egyptians by what I did there, and I brought you out. When I brought your fathers out of Egypt, you came to the sea, and the Egyptians pursued them with chariots and horsemen as far as the Red Sea. But they cried to the LORD for help, and he put darkness between you and the Egyptians; he brought the sea over them and covered them. You saw with your own eyes what I did to the Egyptians. Then you lived in the desert for a long time.

"'I brought you to the land of the Amorites who lived east of the Jordan. They fought against you, but I gave them into your hands. I destroyed them from before you, and you took possession of their land. When Balak son of Zippor, the king of Moab, prepared to fight against Israel, he sent for Balaam son of Beor to put a curse on you. But I would not listen to Balaam, so he blessed you again and again, and I delivered you out of his hand.

"'Then you crossed the Jordan and came to Jericho. The citizens of Jericho fought against you, as did also the Amorites, Perizzites, Canaanites, Hittites, Girgashites, Hivites and Jebusites, but I gave them into your hands. I sent the hornet ahead of you, which drove them out before you—also the two Amorite kings. You did not do it with your own sword and bow. So I gave you a land on which you did not toil and cities you did not build; and you live in them and eat from vineyards and olive groves that you did not plant.'

"Now fear the LORD and serve him with all faithfulness. Throw away the gods your forefathers worshipped beyond the River and in Egypt, and serve the LORD. But if serving the LORD seems undesirable to you, then choose for yourselves this day whom you will serve, whether the gods your forefathers served before you beyond the River, or the gods of the Amorites, in whose land you are living. But as for me and my household, we will serve the LORD."

Then the people answered, "Far be it from us to forsake the LORD and serve other gods! It was the LORD our God himself who brought us and our fathers up out of the land of Egypt, from the land of slavery, and performed those great signs before our eyes. He protected us on our entire journey and among all the nations through which we travelled. And the LORD drove out before us all the nations, including the Amorites, who lived in the land. We too will serve the LORD, because he is our God."

Joshua said to the people, "You are not able to serve the LORD. He is a holy God; he is a jealous God. He will not forgive your rebellion and your sins. If you forsake the LORD and serve foreign gods, he will turn and bring disaster on you and make an end of you, after he has been good to you."

But the people said to Joshua, "No! We will serve the LORD."

The Joshua said, "You are witnesses against yourselves that you have chosen to serve the LORD."

"Yes, we are witnesses," they replied.

"Now then," said Joshua, "throw away the foreign gods that are among you and yield your hearts to the LORD, the God of Israel."

And the people said to Joshua, "We will serve the LORD our God and obey him."

On that day Joshua made a covenant for the people, and there at Shechem he drew up for them decrees and laws. And Joshua recorded these things in the Book of the Law of God. Then he took a large stone and set it up there under the oak near the holy place of the LORD.

"See!" he said to all the people. "This stone will be a witness against us. It has heard all the words the LORD has said to us. It will be a witness against you if you are untrue to your God."

Joshua 24:32 Joseph's bones, which the Israelites had brought up from Egypt, were buried at Shechem in the tract of land that Jacob bought for a hundred pieces of silver from the sons of Hamor, the father of Shechem. This became the inheritance of Joseph's descendants.

Judges 2:1, 2 The angel of the LORD went up from Gilgal to Bokim and said, "I brought you up out of Egypt and led you into the land that I swore to give to your forefathers. I said, 'I will never break my covenant with you, and you shall not make a covenant with the people of this land, but you shall break down their altars.' "

Judges 5:5   The mountains quaked before the LORD, the One of Sinai, before the LORD, the God of Israel.

Ruth 4:3, 4, 9, 10   The he [Boaz] said to the kinsman-redeemer, "Naomi, who has come back from Moab, is selling the piece of land that belonged to our brother Elimelech. I thought I should bring the matter to your attention and suggest that you buy it in the presence of these seated here and in the presence of the elders of my people. If you will redeem it, do so. But if you will not, tell me, so that I will know. For no-one has the right to do it except you, and I am next in line."

Then Boaz announced to the elders and all the people, "Today you are witnesses that I have bought from Naomi all the property of Elimelch, Kilion and Mahlon. I have also acquired Ruth the Moabitess, Mahlon's widow, as my wife, in order to maintain the name of the dead with his property, so that his name will not disappear from among his family or from the town records. Today you are witnesses!"

I Samuel 18:3   And Jonathon made a covenant with David because he loved him as himself.

I Samuel 20:8   As for you, show kindness to your servant, for you have brought him into a covenant with you before the LORD.

II Samuel 23:5   Is not my house right with God? Has he not made with me an everlasting covenant, arranged and secured in every part?

II Samuel 24:16-23   When the angel stretched out his hand to destroy Jerusalem, the LORD was grieved because of the calamity and said to the angel who was afflicting the people, "Enough! Withdraw your hand." The angel of the LORD was then at the threshing-floor of Araunah the Jebusite.

When David saw the angel who was striking down the people, he said to the LORD, "I am the one who has sinned and done wrong, These are but sheep. What have they done? Let your hand fall upon me and my family."

On that day Gad went to David and said to him, "Go up and build an altar to the LORD on the threshing-floor of Araunah the Jebusite." So David went up, as the LORD had commanded through Gad. When Araunah looked and saw the king and his men coming towards him, he went out and bowed down before the king with his face to the ground.

Araunah said, "Why has my lord the king come to his servant?"

"To buy your threshing-floor," David answered, "so that I can build an altar to the_LORD, that the plague on the people may be stopped."

Araunah said to David, "Let my lord the king take whatever pleases him and offer it up. Here are oxen for the burnt offering, and here are the threshing-sledges and the ox yokes for the wood. O king, Araunah gives all this to the king." Araunah also said to him, "May the LORD your God accept you."

II Samuel 24:24, 25 But the king replied to Araunah, "No, I insist on paying you for it, I will not sacrifice to the LORD my God burnt offerings that cost me nothing."

So David bought the threshing-floor and the oxen and paid fifty shekels of silver for them. David built an altar to the LORD there and sacrificed burnt offerings and fellowship offerings. Then the LORD answered prayer on behalf of the land, and the plague on Israel was stopped.

I Kings 8:23 O LORD, God of Israel, there is no God like you in heaven above or on earth below—you who keep your covenant of love with your servants who continue wholeheartedly in your way.

I Kings 11:11 So the LORD said to Solomon, "Since this is your attitude and you have not kept my covenant and my decrees, which I commanded you, I will most certainly tear the kingdom away from you and give it to one of your subordinates."

II Kings 13:23 But the LORD was gracious to them and had compassion and showed concern for them because of his covenant with Abraham, Isaac and Jacob. To this day he has been unwilling to destroy them or banish them from his presence.

II Kings 17:15 They rejected his decrees and the covenant he had made with their fathers and the warnings he had given them. They followed worthless idols and themselves became worthless.

II Kings 17:38 Do not forget the covenant I have made with you, and do not worship other gods.

II Kings 23:3 The King stood by the pillar and renewed the covenant in the presence of the LORD—to follow the LORD and keep his commands, regulations and decrees with all his heart and all his soul, thus confirming the words of the covenant written in this book. Then all the people pledged themselves to the covenant.

I Chronicles 16:15-18 He remembers his covenant for ever, the word he commanded, for a thousand generations, the covenant he made with Abraham, the oath he swore to Isaac. He confirmed it to Jacob as a decree, to Israel as an everlasting covenant: "To you I will give the land of Canaan as the portion you will inherit."

I Chronicles 22:1 Then David said, "The house of the LORD God is to be here, and also the altar of burnt offerings for Israel."

II Chronicles 3:1 Then Solomon began to build the temple of the LORD in Jerusalem on Mount Moriah, where the LORD had appeared to his father David. It was on the threshing-floor of Araunah [Ornan] the Jebusite, the place provided by David.

II Chronicles 6:14 O LORD, God of Israel, there is no God like you in the heaven or earth—you keep your covenant of love with your servants who continue wholeheartedly in your way.

II Chronicles 13:5 Don't you know that the LORD, the God of Israel, has given the kingship of Israel to David and his descendants for ever by a covenant of salt?

II Chronicles 21:7   Nevertheless, because of the covenant the LORD had made with David, the LORD was not willing to destroy the house of David. He had promised to maintain a lamp for him and his descendants for ever.

II Chronicles 34:31   The king stood by his pillar and renewed the covenant in the presence of the LORD—to follow the LORD and keep his commands, regulations and decrees with all his heart and all his soul, and to obey the words of the covenant written in this book.

Nehemiah 1:5   O LORD, God of heaven, the great and awesome God, who keeps his covenant of love with those who love him and obey his commands,

Nehemiah 9:8   You found his [Abraham] heart faithful to you, and you made a covenant with him to give his descendants the land of the Canaanites, Hittites, Amorites, Perizites, Jebusites and Girgashites. You have kept your promise because you are righteous.

Nehemiah 9:32   Now therefore, O our God, the great, mighty and awesome God, who keeps his covenant of love, ...

Psalm 25:12-14   Who, then, is the man that fears the LORD? He will instruct him in the way chosen for him. He will spend his days in prosperity, and his descendants will inherit the land. The LORD confides in those who fear him; and he makes his covenant known to them.

Psalm 37:22   Those the LORD blesses will inherit the land, but those he curses will be cut off.

Psalm 37:34   Wait for the LORD and keep his way. He will exalt you to inherit the land; when the wicked are cut off, you will see it.

Psalm 39:12   Hear my prayer, O LORD, listen to my cry for help; be not deaf to my weeping. For I dwell with you as an alien, a stranger, as all my fathers were.

Psalm 50:5 Gather me my consecrated ones, who made a covenant with me by sacrifice.

Psalm 50:16 But to the wicked, God says: "What right have you to recite my laws or take my covenant on your lips?"

Psalm 69:35, 36 ...for God will save Zion and rebuild the cities of Judah. Then people will settle there and possess it; the children of his servants will inherit it, and those who love his name will dwell there.

Psalm 74:20 Have regard for your covenant, because haunts of violence fill the dark places of the land.

Psalm 78:55 He drove out the nations before them and allotted their lands to them as an inheritance; he settled the tribes of Israel in their homes.

Psalm 87:1-7 He has set his foundation on the holy mountain; the LORD loves the gates of Zion more than all the dwellings of Jacob. Glorious things are said of you, O city of God: "I will record Rahab and Babylon among those who acknowledge me—Philistia too, and Tyre, along with Cush—and will say, 'This one was born in Zion' "

Indeed of Zion it will be said, "This one and that one were born in her and the Most High himself will establish her." The LORD will write in the register of the peoples: "This one was born in Zion." Selah

As they make music they will sing, "All my fountains are in you."

Psalm 89:3, 4 You said, "I have made a covenant with my chosen one, I have sworn to David my servant, 'I will establish your line for ever and make your throne firm through all generations.' "

Psalm 89:28 I will maintain my love to him for ever, and my covenant with him will never fail.

Psalm 89:34 I will not violate my covenant or alter what my lips have uttered.

Psalm 103:17, 18 But from everlasting to everlasting the LORD's love is with those who fear him, and his righteousness with their children's children—with those who keep his covenant and remember to obey his precepts.

Psalm 105:8-11 He remembers his covenant for ever, the word he commanded, for a thousand generations, the covenant he made with Abraham, the oath he swore with Isaac. He confirmed it to Jacob as a decree, to Israel as an everlasting covenant: "To you I will give this land of Canaan as the portion you will inherit."

Psalm 105:42-44 For he remembered his holy promise given to his servant Abraham. He brought out his people with rejoicing, his chosen ones with shouts of joy; he gave them the lands of the nations, and they fell heir to what others had toiled for; that they might keep his precepts and observe his laws.

Psalm 106:45 …for their sake he remembered his covenant and out of his great love he relented.

Psalm 111:5-7, 9 He provides food for those who fear him; he remembers his covenant for ever. He has shown his people the power of his works, giving them the lands of other nations. The works of his hands are faithful and just; all his precepts are trustworthy. He provided redemption for his people; he ordained his covenant for ever—holy and awesome is his name.

Psalm 135:12 …and he gave their land as an inheritance, an inheritance to his people Israel.

Psalm 136:21, 22 …and gave their land as an inheritance, his love endures for ever. An inheritance to his servant Israel; His love endures for ever.

Isaiah 2:2 In the last days the mountain of the LORD's temple will be established as chief among the mountains; it will be raised above the hills, and all nations will stream into it.

Isaiah 14:1 The LORD will have compassion on Jacob; once again he will choose Israel and will settle them in their own land. Aliens will join them and unite with the house of Jacob.

Isaiah 19:19-25 In that day there will be an altar to the LORD in the heart of Egypt, and a monument to the LORD at its border. It will be a sign and a witness to the LORD Almighty in the land of Egypt. When they cry out to the LORD because of their oppressors, he will send them a savior and defender, and he will rescue them. So the LORD will make himself known to the Egyptians, and in that day they will acknowledge the LORD. They will worship with sacrifices and grain offerings; they will make vows to the LORD and keep them. The LORD will strike Egypt with a plague; he will strike them and heal them. They will turn to the LORD, and he will respond their pleas and heal them.

In that day there will be a highway from Egypt to Assyria. The Assyrians will go to Egypt and the Egyptians to Assyria. The Egyptians and Assyrians will worship together. In that day Israel will be the third, along with Egypt and Assyria, a blessing on the earth. The LORD Almighty will bless them, saying, "Blessed be Egypt my people, Assyria my handiwork, and Israel my inheritance."

Isaiah 42:6, 7 I, the LORD, have called you in righteousness; I will take hold of your hand. I will keep you and will make you to be a covenant for the people and a light for the Gentiles, to open eyes that are blind, to free captives from prison and to release from the dungeon those who sit in darkness.

Isaiah 49:8, 9 This is what the LORD says: "In the time of my favor I will answer you, and in the day of salvation I will help you; I will keep you and will make you to be a covenant for the people, to restore the land and to reassign its desolate inheritances, to say to the captives, 'Come out,' and to those in darkness, 'Be free!'

Isaiah 51:1-3 Listen to me, you who pursue righteousness and who seek the LORD: Look to the rock from which you were cut and to the quarry from which you were hewn; look to Abraham, your father, and to Sarah, who gave you birth. When I called him he was but one, and I blessed him and made him many. The LORD will surely comfort Zion and will look with compassion on all her ruins; He will make her deserts like Eden, her wastelands like the garden of the LORD. Joy and gladness will be found in her, thanksgiving and the sound of singing.

Isaiah 54:2, 3 Enlarge the place of your tent, stretch your tent curtains wide, do not hold back; lengthen your cords, strengthen your stakes. For you will spread out to the right and to the left; your descendants will dispossess nations and settle in their desolate cities.

Isaiah 54:10 "Though the mountains be shaken and the hills removed, yet my unfailing love for you will not be shaken nor my covenant of peace be removed," says the LORD, who has compassion on you.

Isaiah 55:3 Give ear and come to me; hear me, that your soul may live. I will make an everlasting covenant with you, my faithful love promised to David.

Isaiah 56:4, 5 This is what the LORD says: "To the eunuchs who keep my Sabbaths, who choose what pleases me and hold fast my covenant—to them I will give within my temple and its walls a memorial and a name better than sons and daughters; I will give them an everlasting name that will not be cut off.

Isaiah 56:6, 7 And foreigners who bind themselves to the LORD to serve him, to love the name of the LORD, and to worship him, all who keep the Sabbath without desecrating it and who hold fast to my covenant—these I will bring to my holy mountain and give them joy in my house of prayer. Their burnt offerings and sacrifices will be accepted on my altar; for my house will be called a house of prayer for all nations.

Isaiah 59:21 "As for me, this is my covenant with them," says the LORD. "My spirit, who is on you, and my words that I have put in your mouth will not depart from your mouth, or from the mouths of your children, or from the mouths of their descendants from this time on and forever," says the LORD.

Isaiah 61:8 For I, the LORD, love justice; I hate robbery and iniquity. In my faithfulness I will reward them and make an everlasting covenant with them.

Isaiah 62:4, 5 No longer will they call you Deserted, or name your land Desolate. But you will be called Hephzibah [my delight is in her], and your land Beulah [married]; for the LORD will take delight in you, and your land will be married. As a young man marries a maiden, so will your sons marry you; as a bridegroom rejoices over his bride, so will your God rejoice over you.

Isaiah 65:9 I will bring forth descendants from Jacob, and from Judah those who will possess my mountains; my chosen people will inherit them, and there will my servants live.

Jeremiah 14:21 For the sake of your name do not despise us; do not dishonor your glorious throne. Remember your covenant with us and do not break it.

Jeremiah 16:15 For I will restore them to the land I gave to their forefathers.

Jeremiah 30:3 "The days are coming [and are here]," declares the LORD, "when I will bring my people Israel and Judah back from captivity and restore them to the land I gave to their forefathers to possess," says the LORD.

Jeremiah 31:5 Again you will plant vineyards on the hills of Samaria; the farmers will plant them and enjoy their fruit.

Jeremiah 31:30-34 "The time is coming," declares the LORD, "when I will make a new covenant with the house of Israel and with the house of Judah. It will not be like the covenant I made with their forefathers when I took them by the hand to lead them out of Egypt, because they broke my covenant, through I was a husband to them," declares the LORD. "This is the covenant that I will make with the house of Israel after that time," declares the LORD. "I will put my law in their minds and write it on their hearts. I will be their God and they will be my people. No longer will a man teach his neighbor, or a man his brother, saying, 'Know the LORD,' because they will all know me, from the least to the greatest," declares the LORD. "For I will forgive their wickedness and will remember their sins no more."

Jeremiah 32:6-8 "Hanamel son of Shallum your uncle is going to come to you and say, 'Buy my field at Anathoth [8km NE of Jerusalem], because as nearest relative it is your right and duty to buy it.'" Jeremiah said, "The word of the LORD came to me: Hanamel son of Shallum your uncle is going to come to you and say, 'Buy my field at Anathoth in the territory of Benjamin. Since it is your right to redeem it and possess it, buy it for yourself."

Jeremiah 32:22 You [Sovereign LORD] gave them this land you had sworn to give their forefathers, a land flowing with milk and honey.

Jeremiah 32:40, 41 I will make an everlasting covenant with them: I will never stop doing good to them, and I will inspire them to fear me, so that they will never turn away from me. I will rejoice in doing them good and will assuredly plant them in this land with all my heart and soul.

Jeremiah 32:44 "Fields will be bought for silver, and deeds will be signed, sealed and witnessed in the territory of Benjamin, in the villages around Jerusalem, in the towns of Judah and in the towns of the hill country, of the western foothills and of the Negev, because I will restore their fortunes, declares the LORD."

Jeremiah 33:8 I will cleanse them from all the sin they have committed against me and will forgive their sins of rebellion against me.

147

Jeremiah 33:11 "I will restore the fortunes of the land as they were before," says the LORD.

Jeremiah 33:20, 21 "This is what the LORD says: 'If you can break my covenant with the day and my covenant with the night, so that day and night no longer come at their appointed time, then my covenant with David my servant—and my covenant with the Levites who are priests ministering before me—can be broken and David will no longer have a descendant to reign on his throne.' "

Jeremiah 33:25, 26 This is what the LORD says: "If I have not established my covenant with day and night and the fixed laws of heaven and earth, then I will reject the descendants of Jacob and David my servant and will not choose one of his sons to rule over the descendants of Abraham, Isaac and Jacob. For I will restore their fortunes and have compassion on them."

Jeremiah 50:5 They will ask the way to Zion and turn their faces towards it. They will come and bind themselves to the LORD in an everlasting covenant that will not be forgotten.

Ezekiel 16:8 Later I passed by, and when I looked at you and saw that you were old enough for love, I spread the corner of my garment over you and covered your nakedness. I gave you my solemn oath and entered into a covenant with you, declares the Sovereign LORD, and you became mine.

Ezekiel 16:59-63 This is what the Sovereign LORD says: I will deal with you as you deserve, because you have despised my oath by breaking the covenant. Yet I will remember the covenant I made with you in the days of your youth, and I will establish an everlasting covenant with you. Then you will remember your ways and be ashamed when you receive your sisters, both those who are older than you and those who are younger. I will give them to you as daughters, but not on the basis of my covenant with you. So I will establish my covenant with you, and you will know that

I am the LORD. Then when I have made atonement for you for all you have done, you will remember and be ashamed and never again open your mouth because of your humiliation, declares the Sovereign LORD.

Ezekiel 20:37, 38 I will take note of you as you pass under my rod, and I will bring you into the bond of the covenant. I will purge you of those who revolt against me. Although I will bring them out of the land where they are living, yet they will not enter the land of Israel. Then you will know that I am the LORD.

Ezekiel 28:25 This is what the Sovereign LORD says: When I gather the people of Israel from the nations where they have been scattered, I will show myself holy among them in the sight of the nations. Then they will live in their own land, which I gave to my servant Jacob.

Ezekiel 34:13, 14 I will bring them out from the nations and gather them from the countries, and I will bring them into their own land. I will pasture them on the mountains of Israel, in the ravines and in all the settlements in the land. I will tend them in a good pasture and the mountain heights of Israel will be their grazing land. There they will lie down in the good grazing land, and there they will feed in a rich pasture on the mountains of Israel.

Ezekiel 34:25 I will make a covenant of peace with them and rid the land of wild beasts so that they may live in the desert and sleep in the forests of safety.

Ezekiel 36

"Son of man, prophesy to the mountains of Israel and say, 'O mountains of Israel, hear the word of the LORD. This is what the Sovereign LORD says: The enemy said of you, "Aha! The ancient heights have become our possession." ' Therefore prophesy and say, 'This is what the Sovereign LORD says: Because they ravaged and hounded you from every side so that you became the possession of the rest of the nations and the object of people's malicious talk and slander, therefore, O mountains of Israel, hear the word of the

Sovereign LORD: This is what the Sovereign LORD says to the mountains and the hills, to the ravines and the valleys, to the desolate ruins and the deserted towns that have been plundered and ridiculed by the rest of the nations around you–this is what the Sovereign Lord says: In my burning zeal I have spoken against the rest of the nations, and against Edom, for with glee and with malice in their heart they made my land their own possession so that they might plunder its pasture-land.' Therefore prophesy concerning the land of Israel and say to the mountains and hills, to the ravines and valleys: 'This is what the Sovereign LORD says: I speak in my jealous wrath because you have suffered the scorn of the nations. Therefore this is what the Sovereign LORD says: I swear with uplifted hand that the nations around you will also suffer scorn.

"'But you, O mountains of Israel, will produce branches and fruit for my people Israel, for they will soon come home. I am concerned for you and will look on you with favor; you will be ploughed and sown, and I will multiply the number of people upon you, even the whole house of Israel. The towns will be inhabited and the ruins rebuilt. I will increase the number of men and animals upon you and they will be fruitful and become numerous. I will settle people on you as in the past and will make you prosper more than before. Then you will know that I am the LORD I will cause people, my people Israel, to walk upon you. They will posses you, and you will be their inheritance; you will never again deprive them of their children.

"'This is what the Sovereign LORD says: Because people say to you, "You devour men and deprive your nation of its children," therefore you will no longer devour men or make your nation childless, declares the Sovereign LORD. No longer will I make you hear the taunts of the nations, and no longer will you suffer the scorn of the peoples or cause your nation to fall, declares the Sovereign LORD.' "

Again the word of the LORD came to me: "Son of man, when the people of Israel were living in their own land, they defiled it by their conduct and their action. Their conduct was like a woman's monthly uncleanness in my sight. So I poured out my wrath on them because they had shed blood in the land and because they had defiled it with their idols. I dispersed them among nations, and there were scattered through the countries; I judged them according to their conduct and their actions. And wherever they went among the nations they profaned my holy name, for it was said of them, 'These are the LORD's people, and yet they had to leave his land.' I had concern for my holy name, which the house of Israel profaned among the nations where they had gone.

"Therefore say to the house of Israel, 'This is what the Sovereign LORD says: It is not for your sake, O house of Israel, that I am going to do these things, but for the sake of my holy name, which you have profaned among the nations where you have gone. I will show the holiness of my great name, which has been profaned among the nations, the name you have profaned among them. Then the nations will know that I am the LORD declares the Sovereign LORD, when I show myself holy through you before their eyes.

"'For I will take you out of the nations; I will gather you from all the countries and bring you back into your own land. I will sprinkle clean water on you, and you will be clean; I will cleanse you from all your impurities and from all your idols. I will give you a new heart and put a new spirit in you; I will remove from you your heart of stone and give you a heart of flesh. And I will put my Spirit in you and move you to follow my decrees and be careful to keep my laws. You will live in the land I gave to your forefathers; you will be my people, and I will be your God. I will save you from all your uncleanness. I will call for the corn and make it plentiful and will not bring famine upon you. I will increase the fruit of the trees and the crops of the field, so that you will no longer suffer disgrace among the nations because of famine. Then you will remember your evil ways and wicked deeds, and you will loathe yourselves for your sins and detestable practices. I want you to know that I am not doing this for you sake, declares the Sovereign Lord. Be ashamed and disgraced for your conduct, O house of Israel!

"'This is what the Sovereign LORD says: On that day I cleanse you from all your sins, I will resettle your towns, and their ruins will be rebuilt. The desolate land will be cultivated instead of lying desolate in the sight of all who pass through it. They will say, "This land that was laid waste has become like the garden of Eden; the cities that were lying in ruins, desolate and destroyed, are now fortified and inhabited." Then the nations around you that remain will know that I the LORD have replanted what was desolate. I the LORD have spoken, and I will do it.'

"This is what the Sovereign LORD says: Once again I will yield to the plea of the house of Israel and do this for them: I will make their people as numerous as sheep, as numerous as the flocks for offerings at Jerusalem during her appointed feasts. So will the ruined cities be filled with flocks and flocks of people. Then they will know that I am the LORD."

Ezekiel 37:22 I will make them one nation in the land, on the mountains of Israel. There will be one king over them and they will never again be two nations or be divided into two kingdoms.

Ezekiel 37:25, 26 They will live in the land I gave to my servant Jacob, the land where your fathers lived. They and their children and their children's children will live there for ever, and David my servant will be their prince for ever. I will make a covenant of peace with them; it will be an everlasting covenant

Ezekiel 38:8 ...a land that has recovered from war, whose people were gathered from many nations to the mountains of Israel, which had long been desolate. They had been brought out from many nations, and now all of them live in safety.

Ezekiel 43:7 Son of Man, this is the place of my throne and the place of the soles of my feet [the temple]. This is where I will live among the Israelites for ever.

Ezekiel 47:13, 14 These are the boundaries by which you are to divide the land for an inheritance among the twelve tribes of Israel, with two portions for Joseph. You are to divide it equally among them. Because I swore with uplifted hand to give it to your forefathers, this land will become your inheritance.

Ezekiel 47:15-20 This is to be the boundary of the land:
On the north side it will run from the Great Sea by the Hethlon road past Lebo Hamath to Zedad, Berothah and Sibraim (which lies on the border between Damascus and Hamath), as far as Hazer Hatticon,

which is on the border of Hauran. The boundary will extend from the sea to Hazar Enan, along the northern border of Damascus, with the border of Hamath to the north. This will be the north boundary.

On the east side the boundary will run between Hauran and Damascus, along the Jordan between Gilead and the land of Israel, to the eastern sea and as far as Tamar. This will be the east boundary.

On the south side it will run from Tamar as far as the waters of Meribah Kadesh, then along the Wadi of Egypt to the Great sea. This will be the south boundary.

On the west side, the Great Sea will be the boundary to a point opposite Lebo Hamath. This will be the west boundary.

Ezekiel 47:21-23 "You are to distribute this land among yourselves according to the tribes of Israel. You are to allot it as an inheritance for yourselves and for the aliens who have settled among you and who have children. You are to consider them native-born Israelites; along with you they are to be allotted an inheritance among the tribes of Israel. In whatever tribe the alien settles, there you are to give him his inheritance," declares the Sovereign LORD.

Ezekiel 48:1-29

"These are the tribes, listed by name: At the northern frontier, Dan will have one portion; it will follow the Hethlon road to Lebo Hamath; Hazar Enan and the northern Border of Damascus next to Hamath will be part of its border from the east side to the west side.

"Asher will have one portion; it will border the territory of Dan from east to west.

"Naphtali will have one portion; it will border the territory of Asher from east to west.

"Manasseh will have one portion; it will border the territory Naphtali from east to west.

"Ephraim will have one portion; it will border the territory of Manasseh from east to west.

"Reuben will have one portion; it will border the territory of Ephraim from east to west.

"Judah will have one portion; it will border the territory of Reuben from east to west.

"Bordering the territory of Judah from east to west will be the portion you are to present as a special gift. It will be 25,000 cubits wide, and its length from east to west will equal on to the tribal portions; the sanctuary will be the centre of it.

"The special portion you are to offer to the LORD will be 25,000 cubits long and 10,000 cubits wide. This will be the sacred portion for the priests. It will be 25,000 cubits long on the north side, 10,000 cubits wide on the west side, 10,000 cubits wide on the east side and 25,000 cubits long on the south side. In the centre of it will be the sanctuary of the LORD. This will be for the consecrated priests, the Zadokites, who were faithful in serving me and did not go astray as the Levites did when the Israelites went astray. I will be a special gift to them from the sacred portion for the land, a most holy portion, bordering the territory of the Levites.

"Alongside the territory of the priests, the Levites will have an allotment 25,000 cubits long and 10,000 cubits wide. Its total length will be 25,000 cubits and its width 10,000 cubits. They must not sell or exchange any of it. This is the best of the land, and must not pass into other hands, because it is holy to the LORD.

"The remaining area, 5,000 cubits wide and 25,000 cubits long, will be for the common use of the city, for houses and for pasture-land. The city will be in the centre of it and will have these measurements: the north side 4,500 cubits, the south side 4,500 cubits, the east side 4,500 cubits, and the west side 4,500 cubits. The pasture-land for the city will be 250 cubits on the north, 250 cubits on the south, 250 cubits on the east, and 250 cubits on the west. What remains of the area, bordering on the sacred portion and running the length of it, will be 10,000 cubits on the east side and 10,000 cubits on the west side. Its produce will supply food for the workers of the city. The workers from the city who farm it will come from all the tribes of Israel. The entire portion will be a square, 25,000 cubits on each side. As a special gift you will set aside the sacred portion, along with the property of the city.

"What remains on both sides of the area formed by the sacred portion and the city property will belong to the prince. It will extend eastward from the 25,000 cubits of the sacred portion to the eastern border, and westward from the 25,000 cubits to the western border. Both these areas running the length of the tribal portions will belong to the prince, and the sacred portion with the temple sanctuary will be in

154

the centre of them. So the property of the Levites and the property of the city will lie in the centre of the area that belongs to the prince. The area belonging to the prince will lie between the border of Judah and the border of Benjamin.

"As for the rest of the tribes: Benjamin will have one portion; it will extend from the east side to the west side.

"Simeon will have one portion; it will border the territory of Benjamin from the east to west.

"Issachar will have one portion; it will border the territory of Simeon from east to west.

"Zeblun will have one portion; it will border the territory of Issachar from east to west.

"Gad will have one portion; it will border the territory of Zeblun from east to west.

"The southern boundary of Gad will run south from Tamar to the waters of Meribah Kadesh, then along the Wadi of Egypt to the Great Sea.

"This is the land you are to allot as an inheritance to the tribes of Israel, and these will be their portions," declares the Sovereign LORD.

Daniel 9:4-6 O Lord, the great and awesome God, who keeps his covenant of love with all who love him and obey his commands, we have sinned and done wrong. We have been wicked and have rebelled; we have turned away from your commands and laws. We have not listened to your servants the prophets, who spoke in your name to our kings, our princes and our fathers, and to all the people of the land.

Hosea 2:18 In that day I will make a covenant for them with the beasts of the field and the birds of the air and the creatures that move along the ground. Bow and sword and battle I will abolish from the land, so that all may lie down in safety.

Hosea 2:23 I will plant her for myself in the land; I will show my love to the one I called 'Not my loved one.' I will say to those called 'Not my people,' 'You are my people;' and they will say, 'You are my God.'

Joel 2:18 The LORD will be jealous for his land and take pity on his people.

Joel 3:1, 2 In those days and at that time, when I restore the fortunes of Judah and Jerusalem, I will gather all nations and bring them down to the Valley of Jehoshaphat. There I will enter into judgement against them concerning my inheritance, my people Israel, for they scattered my people among the nations and divided up my land.

Joel 3:18 In that day the mountains will drip new wine, and the hills will flow with milk; all the ravines of Judah will run with water.

Amos 9:13, 15 "The days are coming," declares the LORD, "when the reaper will be overtaken by the ploughman and the planter by the one treading the grapes. New wine will drip from the mountains and flow from all the hills. I will plant Israel in their own land, never again to be uprooted from the land I have given them."

Obadiah 1:19 People from the Negev will occupy the mountains of Esau, and people from the foothills will possess the land of the Philistines. They will occupy the fields of Ephraim and Samaria, and Benjamin will possess Gilead.

Obadiah 1:21 Deliverers will go up on Mount Zion to govern the mountains of Esau. And the kingdom will be the LORD's.

Micah 4:1, 2 In the last days the mountain of the LORD's temple will be established as chief among the mountains; it will be raised above the hills, and peoples will stream into it. Many nations will come and say, "Come let us go up to the mountain of the LORD, to the house of the God of Jacob. He will teach us his ways, so that we may walk in his paths." The law will go out from Zion, the word of the LORD from Jerusalem.

Zechariah 2:12 The LORD will inherit Judah as his portion in the holy land and will again choose Jerusalem.

Zechariah 9:11 As for you, because of the blood of my covenant with you, I will free the prisoners from the waterless pit.

PART V

Towards Peace:
What is God's Plan

Chapter 13

Seven Middle East Peace Plans

1   ISLAMIC ARAB PEACE PLAN

2   ARAB PALESTINIAN PEACE PLAN

3   GENEVA ACCORD

4   THE NATIONS PEACE PLAN: THE ROAD MAP
    USA, Russia, United Nations, European Union

5   ISRAEL-JEWISH BIBLICAL PEACE PLAN:
    Elon Initiative

6   JORDAN-ISRAEL-PALESTINE CONFEDERATION:
    Prince Hassan bin-Talal Proposal

7   ISRAEL-SONS OF ABRAHAM PEACE PLAN:
    A Biblical Road Map of Reconciliation

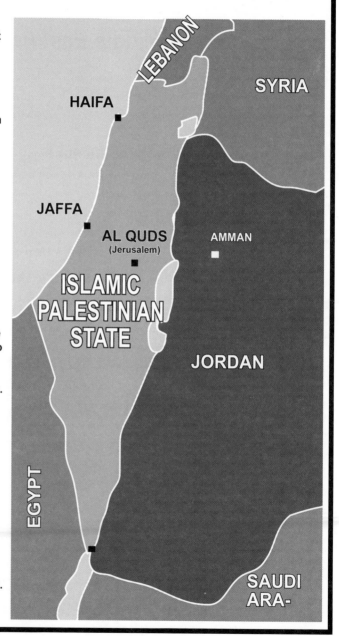

Plan 1

Islamic Arab Peace Plan

Israel ceases to exist as a nation. The word Islam means subjection and submission. Islam was born out of rebellion against the Covenant God of Israel and the Abrahamic covenants made with Abraham, Isaac, and Jacob whose name was changed to Israel.

Muslims worship a false moon god, who in the Koran says that Ishmael, not Isaac. Consequently, the ultimate Islamic Peace Plan says: All of Israel becomes an Islamic Palestinian State as part of the center of an Islamic world. Examples of this are Saudi Arabia and Iran.

LEBANON

SYRIA

HAIFA

JAFFA

AL QUDS
(Jerusalem)

AMMAN

ISLAMIC PALESTINIAN STATE

JORDAN

EGYPT

SAUDI ARA-

Plan 2

Arab Palestinian Peace Plan

A nation under Palestinian Arab rule where Jews could be accepted and without violence against them as in the past in Tunisia or Morocco.

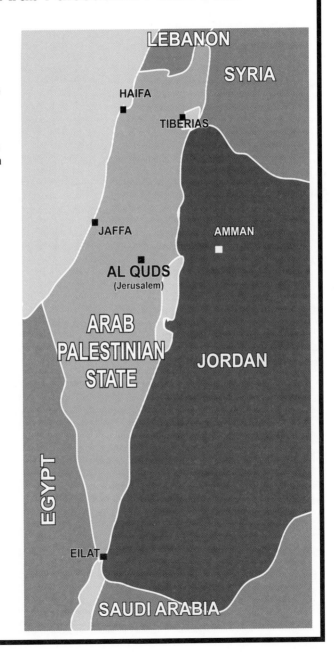

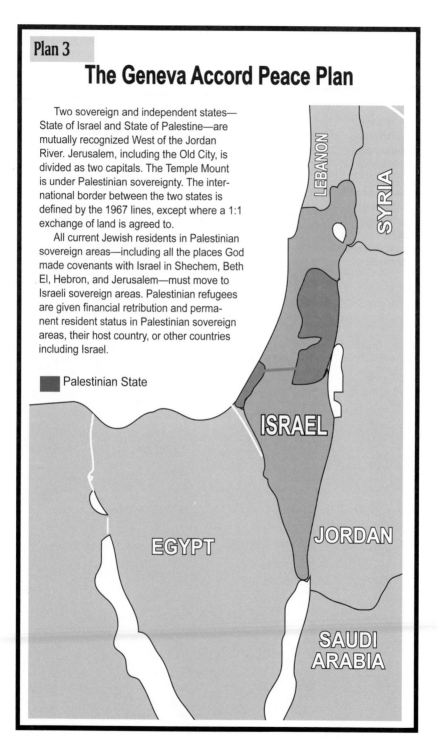

Plan 3

The Geneva Accord Peace Plan

Two sovereign and independent states—State of Israel and State of Palestine—are mutually recognized West of the Jordan River. Jerusalem, including the Old City, is divided as two capitals. The Temple Mount is under Palestinian sovereignty. The international border between the two states is defined by the 1967 lines, except where a 1:1 exchange of land is agreed to.

All current Jewish residents in Palestinian sovereign areas—including all the places God made covenants with Israel in Shechem, Beth El, Hebron, and Jerusalem—must move to Israeli sovereign areas. Palestinian refugees are given financial retribution and permanent resident status in Palestinian sovereign areas, their host country, or other countries including Israel.

■ Palestinian State

LEBANON

SYRIA

ISRAEL

EGYPT

JORDAN

SAUDI ARABIA

Plan 4

The Nations Peace Plan: THE ROAD MAP
USA, Russia, United Nations, European Union

Dividing up land

Plan to divide Israel and build an Islamic Palestinian state in the heartland of Israel.

Joel 3:1, 2 In those days and at that time, when I restore the fortunes of Judah and Jerusalem, I will gather all nations and bring them down to the Valley of Jehoshaphat. There I will enter into judgement against them [the Nations] concerning my inheritance, my people Israel, for they scattered my people among the nations and divided up my land.

The Nations Road Map Peace Plan totally divides the heartland of Israel. This plan proposes to shut down Jewish settlements in the places where God made covenants with the Jews, to uproot and replace the covenantal pillars and foundations of the House of Israel. They want to lay the foundation of an Islamic Palestinian State in these very places in the West Bank of the Jordan —Biblically called Judea and Samaria—the Heartland of Israel.

Two states are partitioned and recognized within the present boundaries of Israel.

Israel
Palestinian
State

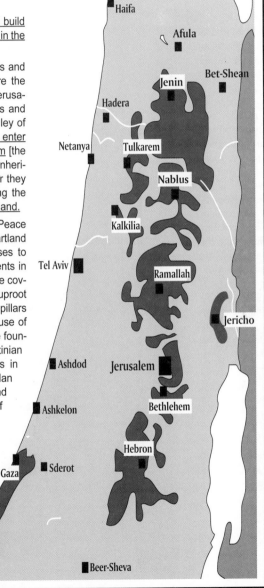

163

Plan 5

Israel-Jewish Biblical Peace Plan: Elon Initiative

This plan stands for Jewish settlements remaining as they are based upon God's Covenant with the Jewish people through Abraham. It stands for Israel remaining as one nation and citizenship of Arabs in Judea, Samaria and the West Bank being transferred to Jordan, which leaders of the plan say IS the Palestinian Arab Islamic State! Interestingly, in 1981 the former King Hussein of Jordan said, "Jordan is Palestine and Palestine is Jordan".

Two states are recognized: Israel on the West side of the Jordan River and one Palestine on the East side of the Jordan River.

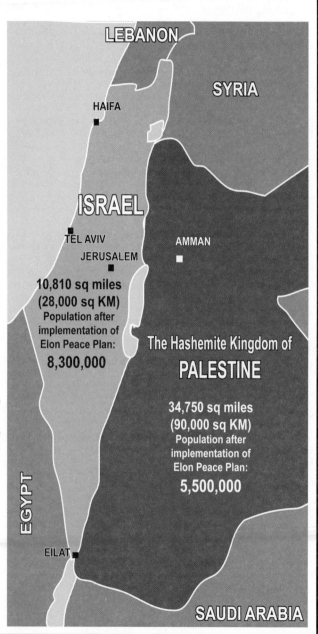

LEBANON

SYRIA

HAIFA

ISRAEL

TEL AVIV

JERUSALEM

AMMAN

10,810 sq miles
(28,000 sq KM)
Population after implementation of Elon Peace Plan:
8,300,000

The Hashemite Kingdom of
PALESTINE

34,750 sq miles
(90,000 sq KM)
Population after implementation of Elon Peace Plan:
5,500,000

EGYPT

EILAT

SAUDI ARABIA

Plan 6   Arab Prince Hassan Peace Proposal

Prince Hassan, former heir to the throne of the Hashemite Kingdom and younger brother to Jordan's deceased monarch, King Hussein, said in a La Stampa interview that Jordan should include all Palestinians. He also said Jordan, Israel, and Palestine should enjoy the same kind of interdependence as there is in the Benelux countries (Holland, Belgium, and Luxembourg). Hassan's proposal seems similar to the Elon Initiative in that Palestinians in Judea and Samaria could be a part of Jordan-Palestine.

In his interview with the Middle East Times, Hassan portrays Ariel Sharon as a pragmatic man, who wants security for his people, but is unable to find a partner on the Palestinian side with whom to conduct negotiations.

Others also support a Jordan-Palestinian confederation. The Palestinian Ambassador to the Arab League, has been quoted in the Middle East Times as saying that a three-state confederation would formalize already strong ties across the Jordan River and that a confederation is the best solution for all—Israelis, Palestinians, and Jordanians—considering Palestinians and Jordanians are one entity. It would solve the refugee and border problems and it would benefit all three economies.

One suggestion not given by Prince Hassan is an Israeli-Jordanian-Palestinian Confederation with Judea and Samaria remaining a part of Israel (the place of Covenant and covenental altars), with an expanded Gaza, as West Palestine, linked with Jordan-East Palestine and supported by Egypt and Israel. If Gaza-West Palestine had their own limited goverment with separate voting, then they would not throw off the political demographics of either Jordan or Israel. With negotiations and prayer, possibilities exist for the Jewish-Elon Initiative and the Arab-Hassan Proposal to connect, as both suggest Palestinian unity and oneness, and Israeli soveriegnty.

165

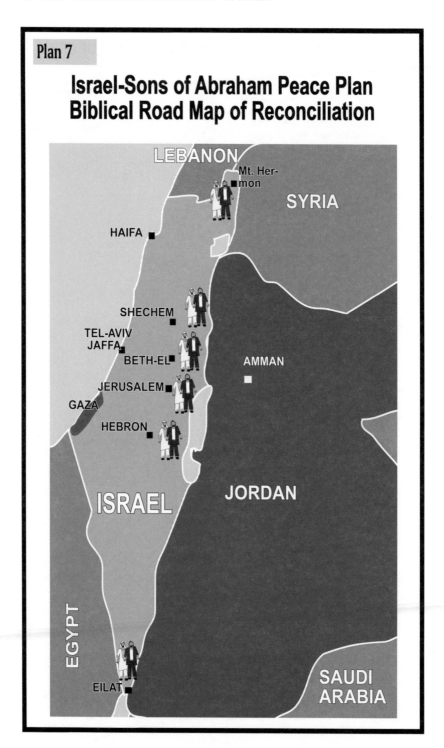

Plan 7 Scripture

This peace plan is based upon God's covenants with Abraham made on Mt. Hermon (Genesis 15), Shechem, Beth El, Hebron, and Jerusalem (Genesis 12, 13, 17, 22) being honored and upheld by Bible-believing Jews and Christians worldwide. This includes Arabs who want to live peacefully with, and throughout, Israel. Jews and Arabs are recognizing and being reconciled to the Abrahamic covenants, the God of Israel, and to one another. This is a biblical road map of reconciliation from Egypt to Eilat to Hebron to Jerusalem to Bethel to Shechem to Mt. Hermon and to Assyria. Arabs who do not want to settle among Jews and live at peace with them could move to Gaza, Jordan, or another nation that would accept them.

In this peace plan all of Israel remains a Jewish State, with Arabs who desire to live there in peace eventually becoming Israeli citizens with Jews, preparing for Messiah's coming. Arab cities in the West Bank-Judea and Samaria would have their own municipalities and mayors and have partial autonomy, but as a part of Israel. The Arab inhabitants could have temporary residency for some years if they personally signed letters saying they recognized the right of the State of Israel to exist, including God's everlasting biblical covenants with Judea and Samaria, and choose to live at peace in and with Israel. After a specified time, citizenship could be given to them if they remain peaceful. Gaza could have autonomy linked with Egypt or linked with Jordan-East Palestine and the nation of Israel, but its inhabitants would not be citizens of Israel.

Ezekiel 47:21-23 "You are to distribute this land among yourselves according to the tribes of Israel. You are to allot it as an inheritance for yourselves and for the aliens who have settled among you and who have children. You are to consider them native-born Israelites; along with you they are to be allotted an inheritance among the tribes of Israel. In whatever tribe the alien settles, there you are to give him his inheritance," declares the Sovereign LORD.

This biblical peace plan of reconciliation stands for Israel to remain as one united nation. There is no Palestinian State in Judea and Samaria mentioned here; however, the majority of Jordanians and all in Gaza are Palestinians. This peace plan highway road map of reconciliation is not only for Israel, but also for the whole Middle East! Under this peace plan according to the population statistics of 2003, sixty-four percent of Israelis would be Jewish and thirty-six percent Arab.

Isaiah 19:23-25 "In that day there will be a highway from Egypt to Assyria. The Assyrians will go to Egypt and the Egyptians to Assyria [Running through Judea and Samaria, Hebron, Beth El, and Shechem]. The Egyptians and Assyrians will worship together. In that day Israel will be the third, along with Egypt and Assyria, a blessing on the earth. The LORD Almighty will bless them, saying, " 'Blessed be Egypt my people, Assyria my handiwork, and Israel my inheritance.' "

Only Messiah's coming will bring ultimate peace, but to the degree we allow the Holy Spirit and Messiah to work through us today we can have shalom/salaam with God and one another.

Isaiah 9:6, 7 "For to us a child is born, to us a son is given, and the government will be on his shoulders. And he will be called Wonderful Counselor, Mighty God, Everlasting Father, Prince of Peace. Of the increase of his government and peace there will be no end. He will reign on David's throne and over his kingdom, establishing and upholding it with righteousness from that time on and FOREVER".

Ezek 43: 1-7 Then the man brought me to the gate facing east, and I saw the glory of the God of Israel coming from the east. His voice was like the roar of rushing waters, and the land was radiant with his glory. The vision I saw was like the vision I had seen when he came to destroy the city and like the vision I had seen by the Kebar River, and I fell face down.

The glory of the LORD entered the temple through the gate facing east. Then the Spirit lifted me up and brought me into the inner court, and the glory of the LORD filled the temple. While the man was standing beside me, I heard someone speaking to me from inside the temple. He said, "Son of Man, this is the place of my throne and the place of the soles of my feet. This is where I will live among the Israelites for ever."

Chapter 14

Pictorial Maps of the Land of Israel: From the Garden of Eden to The New Jerusalem

1   Where was the Garden of Eden (Genesis 2:8-14)?

2   God's Abrahamic Covenants with the People and Whole Land of Israel

3   Abraham's Highway and First Fruit Covenants

4   Land of Israel at time of Twelve Tribes (Joshua 1)

5   Land of Israel at time of Saul, David, and Solomon

6   Land of Israel from 1948 to 1967

7   Land of Israel after Six Day War in 1967 (Ezekiel 36:1-12)

8   Reign of Messiah (Ezekiel 47).
    The Mount of the Lord's Temple Will Be Established and All Nations Will Stream Into It (Ezekiel 43:1-7).

9   Ezekiel's Vision of Jerusalem (Ezekiel 48)

10   New Jerusalem (Isaiah 65:17-19; 66:10-13; Revelation 21:10-21).

Map 1

Where was the Garden of Eden?
(Genesis 2:8-14)

When the sun had set and darkness had fallen, a smoking firepot with a blazing torch appeared and passed between the pieces. On that day the Lord made a covenant with Abram and said, "To your descendants I give this land, from the river of Egypt to the great river, the Euphrates" (Genesis 15: 17,18).

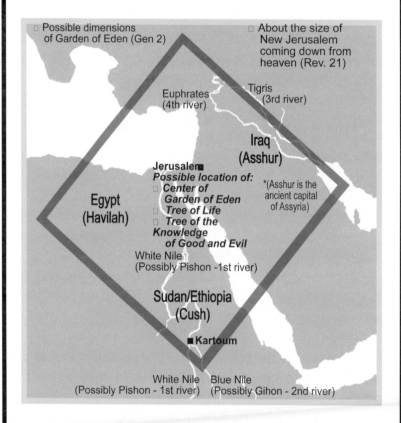

Possible dimensions of Garden of Eden (Gen 2)

About the size of New Jerusalem coming down from heaven (Rev. 21)

Euphrates (4th river)

Tigris (3rd river)

Iraq (Asshur)

Jerusalem
Possible location of:
- Center of Garden of Eden
- Tree of Life
- Tree of the Knowledge of Good and Evil

*(Asshur is the ancient capital of Assyria)

Egypt (Havilah)

White Nile (Possibly Pishon -1st river)

Sudan/Ethiopia (Cush)

Kartoum

White Nile (Possibly Pishon - 1st river)   Blue Nile (Possibly Gihon - 2nd river)

God promised that again Egypt, Israel and Assyria will become a blessing in the midst of the earth (Isaiah 19:23-25). He will also eventually bring the New Jerusalem down from heaven (Isa 65:17-19; 66:10-13 and Revelation 21). The city will be 12,000 stadia (1,400 miles) high, long and wide—a distance that covers the Middle East from the Nile to the Euphrates.

170

Map 2

God's Abrahamic Covenants with the People and Whole Land of Israel

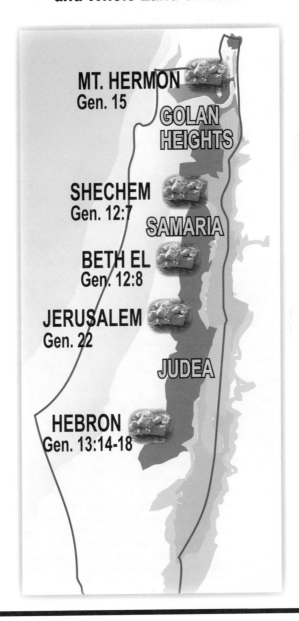

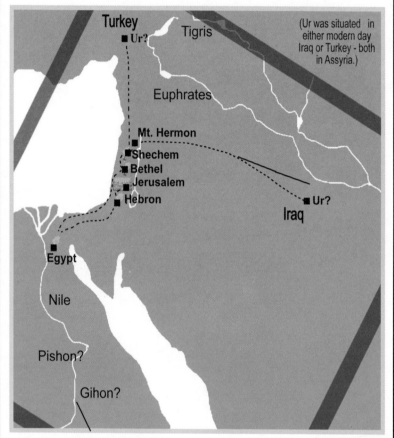

Map 3

Abraham's Highway and First Fruit Covenants

Was Abraham's Journey from Assyria to Israel and Egypt a Walk to Rebuild First Fruits Foundations of the Garden of Eden?

Abraham walked across the Promised Land from Ur in Assyria, through Israel to Egypt and built altars at Shechem and Bethel on his way. He then travelled to Egypt during a famine but returned to build altars at Hebron and Jerusalem (where God stopped him short of sacrificing Isaac (in the center of the Garden)). Abraham was the father of us all—Jews, Arabs and people from all nations are all children of Abraham by faith. He also saw the New Jerusalem coming down out of heaven, which had foundations and whose builder and maker was God (Isaiah 65:17-19, Isaiah 66:10-13, Hebrews 11:8-10).

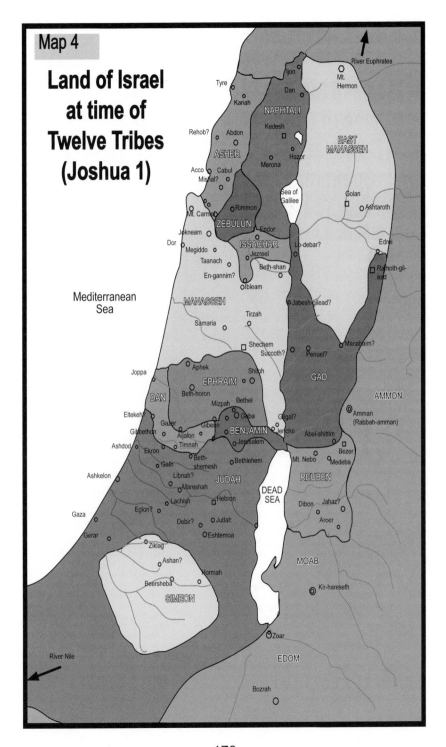

Map 4

Land of Israel
at time of
Twelve Tribes
(Joshua 1)

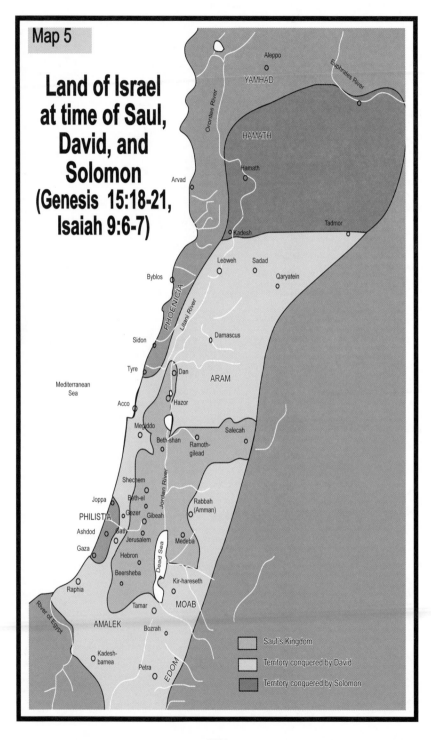

Map 5

Land of Israel at time of Saul, David, and Solomon (Genesis 15:18-21, Isaiah 9:6-7)

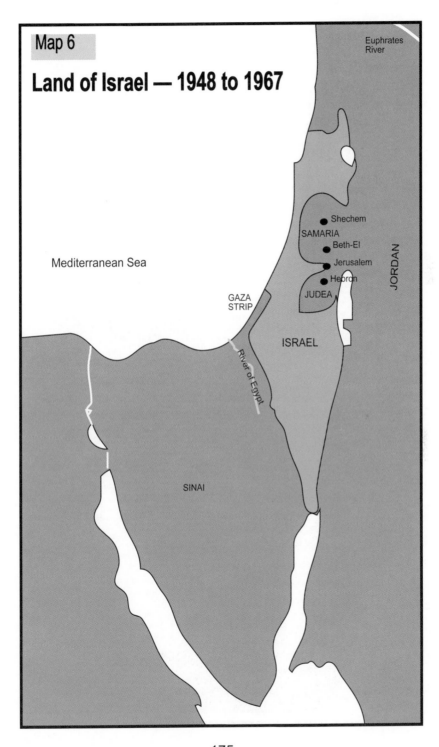

Map 6

Land of Israel — 1948 to 1967

Euphrates
River

Mediterranean Sea

Shechem

SAMARIA

Beth-El

Jerusalem

Hebron

JUDEA

JORDAN

GAZA
STRIP

ISRAEL

River of Egypt

SINAI

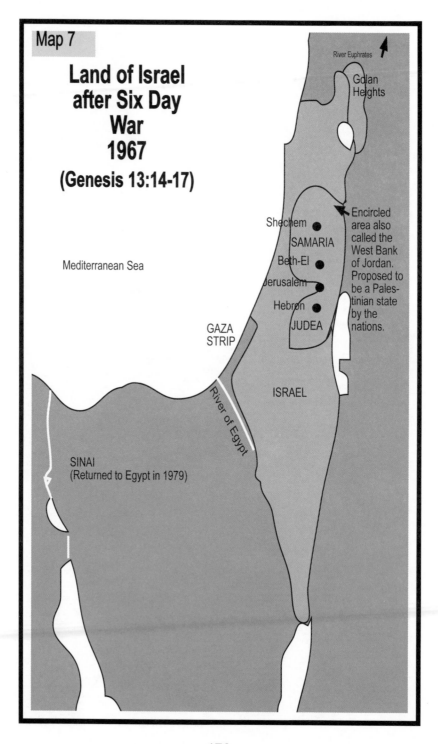

Map 7

Land of Israel after Six Day War 1967

(Genesis 13:14-17)

River Euphrates

Golan Heights

Shechem

SAMARIA

Beth-El

Jerusalem

Hebron

JUDEA

Encircled area also called the West Bank of Jordan. Proposed to be a Palestinian state by the nations.

Mediterranean Sea

GAZA STRIP

River of Egypt

ISRAEL

SINAI
(Returned to Egypt in 1979)

Map 7 Scripture

Ezekiel 36:1-12

Son of man, prophesy to the mountains of Israel and say, "O mountains of Israel, hear the word of the LORD. This is what the Sovereign LORD says: The enemy said of you, 'Aha! The ancient heights have become our possession.' "

Therefore prophesy and say, "This is what the Sovereign LORD says: Because they ravaged and hounded you from every side so that you became the possession of the rest of the nations and the object of people's malicious talk and slander, therefore, O mountains of Israel, hear the word of the Sovereign LORD: This is what the Sovereign LORD says to the mountains and the hills, to the ravines and the valleys, to the desolate ruins and the deserted towns that have been plundered and ridiculed by the rest of the nations around you, this is what the Sovereign Lord says: In my burning zeal I have spoken against the rest of the nations, and against Edom, for with glee and with malice in their heart they made my land their own possession so that they might plunder its pasture-land."

Therefore prophesy concerning the land of Israel and say to the mountains and hills, to the ravines and valleys: "This is what the Sovereign LORD says: I speak in my jealous wrath because you have suffered the scorn of the nations. Therefore this is what the Sovereign LORD says: I swear with uplifted hand that the nations around you will also suffer scorn."

"But you, O mountains of Israel, will produce branches and fruit for my people Israel, for they will soon come home. I am concerned for you and will look on you with favor; you will be ploughed and sown, and I will multiply the number of people upon you, even the whole house of Israel. The towns will be inhabited and the ruins rebuilt. I will increase the number of men and animals upon you and they will be fruitful and become numerous. I will settle people on you as in the past and will make you prosper more than before. Then you will know that I am the LORD. I will cause people, my people Israel, to walk upon you. They will posses you, and you will be their inheritance; you will never again deprive them of their children."

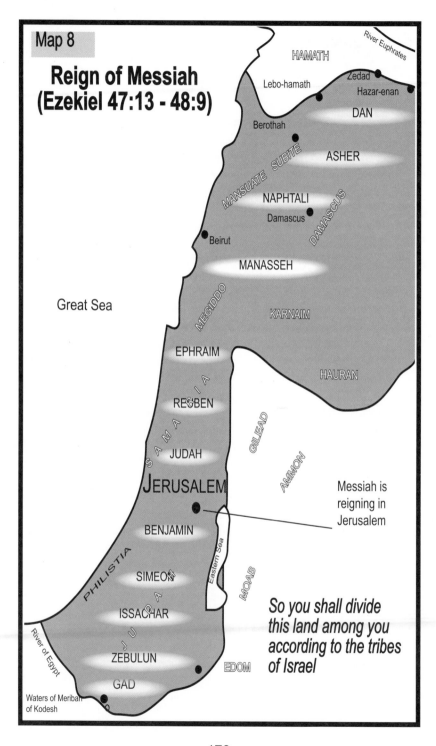

Map 8

Reign of Messiah (Ezekiel 47:13 - 48:9)

River Euphrates

HAMATH

Lebo-hamath

Zedad

Hazar-enan

DAN

Berothah

ASHER

MANSUATE SUBITE

NAPHTALI

Damascus

DAMASCUS

Beirut

MANASSEH

MEGIDDO

Great Sea

KARNAIM

EPHRAIM

S A M A R I A

HAURAN

REUBEN

GILEAD

JUDAH

AMMON

JERUSALEM

Messiah is reigning in Jerusalem

BENJAMIN

PHILISTIA

Eastern Sea

SIMEON

MOAB

J U D A

ISSACHAR

So you shall divide this land among you according to the tribes of Israel

River of Egypt

ZEBULUN

EDOM

GAD

Waters of Meribah of Kodesh

IN THE LAST DAYS THE MOUNTAIN OF THE LORD'S TEMPLE WILL BE ESTABLISHED AND ALL NATIONS WILL STREAM INTO IT. Isaiah 2:1,2

Ezekiel 43:1-7: Then the man brought me to the gate facing east, and I saw the glory of the God of Israel coming from the east. His voice was like the roar of rushing waters, and the land was radiant with his glory. The vision I saw was like the vision I had seen when he came to destroy the city and like the vision I had seen by the Kebar River, and I fell face down.

The glory of the LORD entered the temple through the gate facing east. Then the Spirit lifted me up and brought me into the inner court, and the glory of the LORD filled the temple. While the man was standing beside me, I heard someone speaking to me from inside the temple. He said, "Son of Man, this is the place of my throne and the place of the soles of my feet. This is where I will live among the Israelites for ever."

Map 9

Ezekiel's Vision of Jerusalem (Ezekiel 48)

| Gate of Levi | Gate of Judah | Gate of Reuben |

Gate of Naphtali

Gate of Joseph

Temple

Gate of Asher

Gate of Benjamin

Gate of Gad

Jerusalem

Gate of Dan

| Gate of Zebulun | Gate of Issachar | Gate of Simeon |

Ezekiel 48:30-35 These will be the exits of the city: Beginning on the north side, which is 4,500 cubits long, the gates of the city will be named after the tribes of Israel. The three gates on the north side will be the gate of Reuben, the gate of Judah and the gate of Levi.

On the east side, which is 4,500 cubits long, will be three gates: the gate of Joseph, the gate of Benjamin and the gate of Dan.

On the south side, which measures 4,500 cubits, will be three gates: the gate of Simeon, the gate of Issachar and the gate of Zebulun.

On the west side, which is 4,500 cubits long, will be three gates: the gate of Gad, the gate of Asher and the gate of Naphtali.

The distance all around will be 18,000 cubits. And the name of the city from that time on will be: THE LORD IS THERE. Some Christians believe that the Messiah will reign 1000 years based upon their understanding of Revelation 20:4.

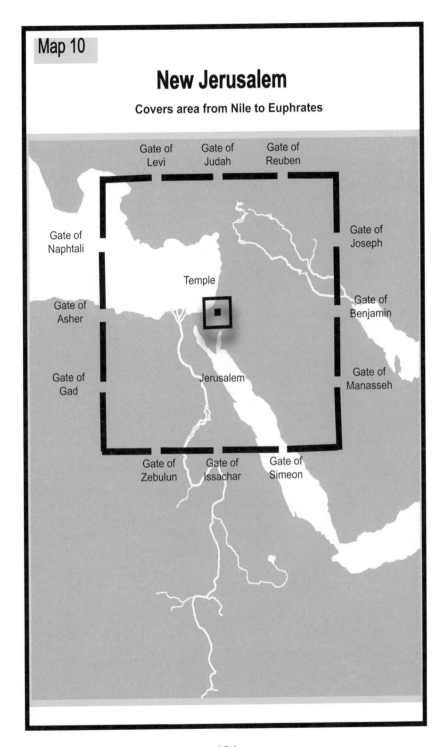

Map 10

New Jerusalem

Covers area from Nile to Euphrates

Gate of Levi

Gate of Judah

Gate of Reuben

Gate of Naphtali

Gate of Joseph

Temple

Gate of Asher

Gate of Benjamin

Jerusalem

Gate of Gad

Gate of Manasseh

Gate of Zebulun

Gate of Issachar

Gate of Simeon

Map 10 Scripture

Isaiah 65:17-19 Behold, I will create new heavens and a new earth. The former things will not be remembered, nor will they come to mind. But be glad and rejoice forever in what I will create, for I will create Jerusalem to be a delight and its people a joy. I will rejoice over Jerusalem and take delight in my people; the sound of weeping and crying will be heard in it no more.

Isaiah 66:10-13 Rejoice with her Jerusalem and be glad for her, all you who love her; rejoice greatly with her, all you who mourn over her. For you will nurse and be satisfied at her comforting breasts; you will drink deeply and delight in her overflowing abundance.

For this is what the LORD says: I will extend peace to her like a river, and the wealth of the nations like a flooding stream; you will nurse and be carried on her arm and dandled on her knees. As a mother comforts a child, so will I comfort you, and you will be comforted over Jerusalem.

In the New (Testament) Covenant it says:

Revelation 21:10-21 And he carried me away in the Spirit to a mountain great and high, and showed me the Holy City, Jerusalem, coming down out of heaven from God. It shone with the glory of God, and its brilliance was like that of a very precious jewel, like a jasper, clear as crystal. It had a great, high wall with twelve gates, and with twelve angels at the gates. On the gates were written the names of the twelve tribes of Israel. There were three gates on the east, three on the north, three on the south and three on the west. The wall of the city had twelve foundations, and on them were the names of the twelve apostles of the Lamb.

The angel who talked with me had a measuring rod of gold to measure the city, its gates and its walls. The city was laid out like a square, as long as it is wide. He measured the city with the rod and found it to be 12,000 stadia [about 1,400 mi or 2,500 KM] in length, and as wide and high as it is long. He measured its wall and it was 144 cubits thick [200 ft or 65 m], by man's measurement, which the angel was using. The wall was made of jasper, and the city of pure gold, as pure as glass. The foundations of the city walls were decorated with every kind of precious stone. The first foundation was jasper, the second sapphire, the third chalcedony, the fourth emerald, the fifth sardonyx, the sixth carnelian, the seventh chrysolite, the eight beryl, the ninth topaz, the tenth chrysoprase, the eleventh, jacinth, and the twelfth amethyst. The twelve gates were twelve pearls, each gate made of a single pearl. The great street of the city was of pure gold, like transparent glass.

182

Appendix

Watchmen's Materials

House of Prayer for All Nations

A collection of 200 nations' redemptive purposes, key 24-hour Watches, and other useful information, A House of Prayer for All Nations is a watchmen's arsenal to help Watchmen proclaim, pray and praise their way through the nations of the earth.

ISBN: 965-7193-09-5   **$14.00**

God's Abrahamic Covenants with Israel & the Church

This book is a biblical road map towards reconciliation that gives prophetic clarity from the Word of God on how God's covenants with the land of Israel, the Jewish people, and the Church are for today and forever.

ISBN: 965-7193-13-3   **$14.00**

Sons of Abraham

Testimonies of Jewish and Arab leaders throughout the last two centuries, prophetic acts and convocations in the last twenty years, and a synopsis of the restoration of the Church in Egypt, Israel, and Assyria, in this book shows how God is preparing the way for fullness.

ISBN: 965-7193-03-6   **$14.00**

183

Prepare the Way for the King of Glory

An in-depth manual for the spiritual map of Jerusalem designed to equip watchmen for their task of praying for Jerusalem and Israel.

ISBN: 965-7193-02-8 $14.00

Let my People Go!

In the return of the Jews to Israel, Tom Hess sees the prophetically promised turning point in history. This book is an impassioned appeal to Jewry worldwide to resume their God-given role as "a light to the nations."

ISBN: 965-7193-12-5 $ 10.00

The Watchmen

In this book, Tom Hess will help you to assume your role as a watchman.

ISBN: 965-7193-00-1 $15.00

Pray for the Peace of Jerusalem

Every believer has an obligation to pray for the peace of Jerusalem. This book explains how.

ISBN: 965-7193-01-x $14.00

LIVE WORSHIP FROM ISRAEL

Music from the All Nations Convocation Jerusalem *All CDs: $15.00 or Casettes: $10.00*

Volume 1 Watchmen's songs performed by the Messianic Community of Reconciliation Worship Team. Many of these songs were written by Tom Hess.

Volume 2 Energetic and passionate Hebrew worship by the Messianic Jewish Beit Avinu Worship Team from Tel Aviv.

Volume 3 James Trumbo and his family in prohetic breakthrough worship.

Volumes 4 and 5 Albums with a truly international flavor, featuring worship leaders like Robin Mark from Ireland, Luke Kaa-Morgan from New Zealand, Rob Stearns from the US and Robert Soetanto from Indonesia on Volume 4; with Barry and Batya Segal from Israel, Scot Ezzy from Australia, Gerson Ortega from Brazil and Lilo Keller from Switzerland on Volume 5.

Prepare the Way for the King of Glory Worship Series.

LIVE WORSHIP from the All Nations Covocation and World Wide Watch Convocation. Includes various artists from around the world.

Sons of Abraham LIVE!

Jews and Arabs worship God together as a blessing in the midst of the earth. 2 Volumes.

Free Watchmen's Materials
for Watchmen and 24-hour Watches

1. **An Individual Watch Log**
2. **A sample sign-up sheet for a 24-hour Watch**
3. **The JHOPFAN Watch and Corporate Prayer Schedule**
4. **Monthly Prophetic Prayer Alert**—up to date aid helping watchmen on the World Wide Watch pray each day for Jerusalem, Israel and the nations.
5. **Addresses of models of 24-hour Watches**—list of Watches and models available
6. ***Jerusalem Watch of the King* Info**—Information about coming to Jerusalem to participate in the *Jerusalem Watch of the King* on the Twelve Gates of Jerusalem.

Contact us if Interested in:

1. **Starting a 24-hour Watch** for Jerusalem, Israel and my city, nation and all nations—Ps 122:6; Jer 29:7; Isa 56; Isa 62
2. **Participating in the *World Wide Watch***
3. **Participating in *Jerusalem Watch of the King***
4. **Bringing a team of Watchmen** to participate in 10-day *Prophetic Prayer Pigramage* or 7-day *Watchmen's Week*
5. **Applying to join the *Jerusalem House of Prayer for All Nations* staff** in Israel—(send resume, photo and pastor's recommendation letter when applying and ask for staff application). Contact us for a list of positions available.
6. **Distributing Watchmen's Materials**
7. **Financially supporting JHOPFAN**

Teaching Tapes
Audio:$4 each, $25 for 7

Video: $15 each, $45 for 5, $75 for 10
Please contact us for a list of our latest teachings.

<u>Checks payable to</u>: ***Jerusalem House of Prayer for All Nations***

<u>or Wire Transfer to U.S. account</u>:

Progressive Vision International General Account #17-103-241,

Riggs National Bank of Washington DC /

Branch #31, Routing #054-00-00-30, (SWIFT: RGGSUS33)

650 Pennsylvania Ave. SE Washington DC 20005 USA,

<u>or Wire Transfer to Singapore account</u>:
DBS Bank, 6 Shenton Way, DBS Building
Singapore 068809;   Swift: DBSSSGSG
Acc. Holder: Thomas Darrell Hess, Acc#: 0010-000017-01-0-022
P.O. Box 31393, Jerusalem 91313, Israel

<u>or Wire Transfer to Swiss account</u>:

Attn: Thomas Hess, Swiss Bank Corporation:

Thunstrasse 4, CH-3110 Munsingen, Switzerland;

CHF#235 FJ 110493.0; USD#235 FJ 110493.1;

EUR#235-PRIV98204.609.3; PC-30-35-9, BC 235

<u>or Wire Transfer to French account</u>:
Progressive Vision International,
Attn. Tom Hess
B.N.P. Chaville Pave des Gardes
Acc: 30004-00180-86106-63

<u>or Wire Transfer to German account</u>:
Thomas Hess
Jerusalem House of Prayer for All Nations
Deutsche Bank, Berlin Branch: 704
Alexanderplatz 6, 10178 Berlin
Bankleitzahl: 100 700 24;   Account #: 1193762 00
IBAN: DE37 1007 0024 0119 3762 00
BIC (SWIFT): DEUTDEDBBER

<u>or Wire Transfer to German account</u>:
All Nations Convocations Jerusalem, Account #375011,

Bank Hapoalim, Branch 12-784, HaHaganah 21, Jerusalem, Israel

(Please designate if for a specific need and send us a copy of your transfer.)

join the
WORLD WIDE WATCH
Surrounding the Throne of the King from the Ends of the Eath

24-hours a day, 7-days a week, 365-days a year the throne of the King, Yeshua, is being surrounded from the ends of the earth. This is the **World Wide Watch**.

Watches are kept by Houses of Prayer, churches, and other communities of prayer and intercession in hundreds of nations worldwide. Every day Watchmen join together with others in their Gates-Gateways for at least two hours at a time. For Example, watchmen in India Vietnam and Papa New Guinea all join in the Golden Gate Watch from 6-8 am Jerusalem time. For Watchmen in India this is 8-10 am Indian time, in Vietnam 11-1 pm Vietnamese time, and for Papa New Guinea 4-6 pm New Guinean time. For ten days Watchmen from all nations come to Jerusalem to keep their watches together in one place at the All Nations Convocation Jerusalem and the World Wide Watch Convocation held between Rosh Hashanah and Yom Kippur every year.

JOIN US FOR THE ANNUAL

ALL NATIONS CONVOCATION JERUSALEM
WORLD WIDE WATCH CONVOCATION
AND
WATCHMEN'S TOUR OF ISRAEL

HIGHLIGHTS INCLUDE

Ten days and nights in Jerusalem.

Focused intercession, worship and teaching from some of the great prophetic and apostolic leaders of this age.

Touring Jerusalem with onsight intercession on the Twelve Gates of Jerusalem.

Celebrating Rosh Hashana and Yom Kippur with the local body of Jewish and Arab beleivrs from Jerusalem, Israel and all the Middle East.

Three days and nights touring the Holy Land guided by professionals to stand with local ministries in prayer, intercede in key locatiotns like the place of the four altars, and worship in the same places Yeshua did.

For more information about specific dates and costs or to request a registration form, please contact us:

www.jhopfan.org
ancj@jhopfan.org
+971-2-6261518
TOLL FREE from the US 1-888-513-9580
Fax +972-2-626-4239

TOM HESS

Called to stand with God for His purposes for Jerusalem, Tom Hess has lived on the peak of the Mount of Olives since 1987 at the Golden Gate House of Prayer with the most direct view possible of the Golden Gate and the Temple Mount. He is the Pastor of the Jerusalem House of Prayer for All Nations and Pastoral Gatekeeper of both the Golden Gate and the Bethany / Bethphage Gate contributing to both the 24-hour Watch at the Jerusalem House of Prayer for All Nations, the Jerusalem Watch of the King, and the World WIde Watch. He is the president of the All Nations Convocation Jerusalem and Progressive Vision Publishing.

Tom Hess is the author of numerous books presenting an authentic view of issues surrounding Israel, Jerusalem, and the Middle East. In his books you will enjoy such topics as God's covenants with the people and land of Israel, reconciliation of Jews and Arabs, Aliyah, and prayer. Tom also travels the world sharing God's heart for the covenant land and the covenant people while encouraging new 24-hour Watches to be birthed.

PROGRESSIVE VISION PUBLISHING

How beautifulupon the mountains are the feet of him that brings good tidings, that publishes peace; that brings good tidings of good, that publishes salvation; that says unto Zion, Thy God reigns! —Isaiah 52:7